Writing Outside Your Comfort Zone

Helping Students Navigate Unfamiliar Genres

CATHY FLEISCHER

SARAH ANDREW-VAUGHAN

Heinemann
Portsmouth, NH

Heinemann
361 Hanover Street
Portsmouth, NH 03801–3912
www.heinemann.com

Offices and agents throughout the world

Library of Congress Cataloging-in-Publication Data
Fleischer, Cathy.
    Writing outside your comfort zone : helping students navigate unfamiliar genres / Cathy Fleischer and Sarah Andrew-Vaughan.
        p.   cm.
    Includes bibliographical references.
    ISBN 13: 978-0-325-01247-6
    ISBN 10: 0-325-01247-4
    1. English language—Composition and exercises—Study and teaching (Secondary).
2. Language arts (Secondary).   3. Literary form.   I. Andrew-Vaughan, Sarah.   II. Title.
LB1631.F613   2009
808'.0420712—dc22   2008037961

Editor: James Strickland
Production: Elizabeth Valway
Cover design: Bernadette Skok
Composition: Cape Cod Compositors, Inc.
Manufacturing: Steve Bernier

Printed in the United States of America on acid-free paper
12 11 10 09 08 VP 1 2 3 4 5

To all the students who have taught us so much

Contents

Foreword

WRITING OUTSIDE YOUR COMFORT
ZONE presents an exciting and innovative new concept—the Unfamiliar
Genre Project (UGP). It's unlike anything I've ever seen before, and yet, as I
read through Fleischer and Andrew-Vaughan's thoughtful discussions and the
wonderfully rich classroom examples, I can't help feeling that the unfamiliar
is actually quite familiar. Certainly this book builds on a pedagogically solid
foundation of inquiry-driven instruction and genre-based study, but there's
more to it than that. The authors' goals for the UGP—student ownership of
the writing process, empowerment of young writers as independent thinkers,
development of sense of self as an independent writer—are goals that echo
through several generations of writing about writing. They are goals that are
stated often, but truly meeting them remains elusive. What is unique and exciting about Fleischer and Andrew-Vaughan's work is that through the UGP
they present a practical, classroom-tested approach that has the capacity to
actually fulfill these promises.

In *Time for Meaning*, Randy Bomer writes, "I don't teach poetry so that my
kids will remember all about writing poems and be able to do it forever. I want
them to develop habits of mind related to learning in a genre, so that they can
learn in whatever genres they need" (1995, 119). The first time I read this comment it resonated so strongly that the hair on my arms stood up. Genre-based

units, properly conceived, shouldn't simply be about teaching a particular structural form (though I've seen too many examples where units are reduced to just that); rather, they need to be opportunities for exploration and reflection that emphasize the importance of process.

When researching and writing my own text, *Thinking Through Genre* (Lattimer 2003), I tried to emphasize the centrality of inquiry in guiding genre-based units. My teacher colleagues and I immersed students in reading and writing within a genre, we encouraged them to consider the interplay between purpose, audience, voice, and structure, we modeled the process of revisiting and reconsidering our own writing, and we provided regular opportunities for metacognitive reflection on the nature of inquiry and the process of writing. But even as we worked, I wondered if, despite all of these opportunities to explore process, it was really enough. I doubted whether students, even after exploring several different genres through such an inquiry-driven approach, would really be able to independently explore and write within an unfamiliar genre on their own.

In the text itself, I gave a nod to the idea that maybe teachers would need to do more. In a section of the introductory chapter outlining the process of genre selection and discussing unit progressions over the course of a year, I suggested that teachers and students "may decide to follow the investigative approach used in genre studies to explore a new genre independently or as part of a small group" (10). This was followed by some lofty words about empowering students to build on their knowledge of process and define for themselves who they want to become as readers and writers. It sounded lovely, and I actually believed that it was important, but, truth be told, I had no idea how to go about achieving such a concept.

Fortunately, Fleischer and Andrew-Vaughan have a very clear understanding of how to engage students in studying unfamiliar genres, and after reading this excellent book, you will too. They begin the text with a thoughtful discussion of theory behind genre studies generally and the Unfamiliar Genre Project in particular. They articulate clear and reasonable goals for the project—the aim is not to have students produce the best exemplar of the genre, but to help them internalize the process of investigating genre and gain the habits of mind and confidence needed to approach writing in new genres and for new purposes. As a former history teacher, I was particularly intrigued by the idea of reconceptualizing an inquiry into genre as a research project in the writing classroom. This approach adds depth to the project and extends its potential impact far beyond the realm of the English language arts classroom.

Fleischer and Andrew-Vaughan then invite us into the classroom. We are introduced to Sarah's class, a wonderfully challenging group of students, and allowed to listen in as Andrew-Vaughan lays the groundwork for the UGP through a series of whole-class inquiries into author blurbs, standardized test writing, and comic writing. These introductory units serve to help students acclimate to the process of genre-based writing. Simultaneously, they provide us, the readers, with clear examples of the priorities that Fleischer and Andrew-Vaughan emphasize in their work. In particular, they illustrate use of what the authors term as the four *Is*—immersion, inquiry, instruction, and integration. These principles are articulated early in the text, come to life in the genre units, and serve to ground and guide the authors' work during the UGP itself.

The highlight of the book is the exploration of the UGP. Although the concept of teaching such a unit may seem overwhelming, Fleischer and Andrew-Vaughan step the reader through the possibilities of teaching unfamiliar genres in a manner that reflects their work in the classroom. Their writing encourages trust, establishes a safe environment for exploring new ideas, allows for questions and adaptations, and provides outstanding models of both their work and the work of their students. We don't just see the final product—though they have included an example of a student's full research binder, an invaluable instructional resource—we also see the work in process. We get to listen in as Sarah responds to students' early efforts and read over students' shoulders as they reflect on their progress. We watch as students grow in their confidence, take ownership over their process, and become more aware of themselves as writers and as individuals. And Fleischer and Andrew-Vaughan provide plenty of practical support as well—including calendars, assignment descriptions, rubrics, and multiple samples of student work. While reading through these chapters, the power and possibility of writing and teaching unfamiliar genres becomes apparent. As I finished the manuscript, I found myself eager to share the book with colleagues, wanting to craft an original piece of microfiction, and excited to try out Fleischer's preservice teacher version of the UGP with my university students.

In many ways, I see this book as the completion of a circle. Authors such as Nancie Atwell, Donald Graves, and Lucy Calkins started a revolution in writing when they encouraged us to recast our classrooms as writing workshops. Encouraged by these pioneers, we moved off the teacher stage and into the role of facilitator, built communities of writers in our classrooms, and provided time in class to plan, draft, revise, and publish.

The genre-based approach grew out of the writing workshop model. Realizing how difficult it was to implement a true workshop, one in which each student focused on her own topic and genre at her own pace, we began to craft genre-based units of study that would engage the whole class. Moving the whole class through a genre unit together allowed us to craft minilessons that were more widely applicable, provided greater opportunities for students to collaborate in their learning, and generally made the workshop logistics more manageable. Many found that stronger writing and stronger writing communities grew out of the genre-focused approach. However, there were risks in focusing exclusively on genre-based units. Students didn't have full ownership over the product or the process. They were reliant on teachers to guide the inquiry, choose the text samples, and model the writing process. For all of the strengths that genre-based writing instruction offered, it failed, even in the best of circumstances, to fully live up to the goals set out by the original architects of the writing workshop.

And this is where the UGP closes the circle. Fleischer and Andrew-Vaughan's work provides a bridge between the strengths of genre-based instruction and the goals of the writing workshop. It builds on the depth of understanding that genre-based units nurture and empowers students to take full ownership over their writing process and product. It provides clear structure and support to guide the inquiry process but resists the temptation to wrest control away from student writers. It fosters a community among writers while simultaneously cultivating each student's sense of self as an individual author. As the examples Fleischer and Andrew-Vaughan provide make clear, the potential results of the UGP are powerful. Students emerged from their inquiry with a deeper understanding of the writing process, more confidence in their ability to engage with new genres, and a redefined sense of themselves as writers.

This work is an important contribution to the field of writing instruction, but it is also a great read. The advice is practical, the resources helpful, and the discussion thought provoking. Fleischer and Andrew-Vaughan are wonderful guides on the journey through the UGP and do for readers exactly what they want us to do for students—they invite us in, earn our trust, and then support us as we take on a new and unfamiliar challenge. Enjoy the journey!

Heather Lattimer
School of Leadership and Education Sciences
University of San Diego

Works Cited

Bomer, Randy. 1995. *Time for Meaning: Crafting Literate Lives in Middle and High School.* Portsmouth, NH: Heinemann.

Lattimer, Heather. 2003. *Thinking Through Genre: Units of Study in Reading and Writing Workshop*, 4-12. Portland, ME: Stenhouse.

Preface

Teaching and Learning the Unfamiliar

IMAGINE THIS CLASSROOM SCENARIO: A group of thirty high school students is hard at work in a writing workshop classroom, each student pursuing an individual genre—finding and reading examples of that genre, creating a list of characteristics of that genre, writing his own piece in the genre, and reflecting on what he has learned about the genre as a result of his individual study. Maria, for example, is working on creating a children's book, a story that she wants to make sure speaks to an audience of parents and children. She reads numerous examples of children's books, looking carefully at how the authors of those books craft a relationship between the words and the pictures and wondering how she might do the same in her own book. Nikitha is trying to figure out how to write a college entrance essay, skimming the websites of various colleges to identify the kinds of essay prompts they offer, looking through books from various sources with sample successful college essays, and trying to figure out how her own sense of self can be conveyed through this genre. Melissa is working on a sonnet; Theresa is writing song lyrics; Patrick is writing a sports story.

Now imagine part two of this scenario: The genres these students have chosen for their writing are not the ones that they are the *most* familiar with, as is typical of many writing workshops. Rather, these students are immersing themselves in those genres that they feel the *least* familiar with. The students, for the purposes of this assignment, are writing in genres that are not particularly comfortable for them, in genres they name as unfamiliar, challenging, or maybe just plain scary. Zac tells us why he selected a music review as his genre to study: "I love to listen to music and read reviews of CDs to know which ones to buy, but I never thought I would be any good at actually writing one. I thought this project could help me analyze and interpret an artist or album better; that way I could give my friends better input on what CD to buy other than 'Yeah, it has some good songs on it.'" Theresa chose the genre of song lyrics because it's something she's always wanted to try, but wasn't quite sure how to do: "I've always wanted to write my own lyrics for a song but really never could finish it, or really did not know where to start or end." Nikitha has immersed herself in a genre that seems particularly scary to her, the college entrance essay: "Writing a college essay was something I'd been nervous about for years."

The two of us have been working with students on this concept of "genres that challenge us" for several years, an approach that has resulted in a unit of study we collaborated to create, called the Unfamiliar Genre Project. And who are we? Sarah is an English teacher, more than ten years into her career at a diverse high school in a small city. Cathy, a former high school teacher, is now an English educator at a nearby university. Over the years we've developed a wonderful partnership: Cathy's preservice teachers work with Sarah's high school students; Sarah is part of a teacher-research group Cathy facilitates; the two of us talk about teaching and literacy and reform (and life) all the time; and for one wonderful semester, Cathy was able to spend three days a week as a participant observer in one of Sarah's classes as we rolled out a curriculum that centered on the concepts introduced in this book.

Over the last few years of partnership, as we've thought and rethought, refined and revised, we've had the chance to work on the Unfamiliar Genre Project with students at various grade levels and in various kinds of classrooms, from Cathy's preservice teachers at the university to Sarah's composition and literature classes at the high school. We've worked with students in accelerated classes and students in heterogeneous groups, students who knew a lot about writing and students who were uneasy writers. And while our approaches to the Unfamiliar Genre Project have varied somewhat depending on these circumstances and contexts, the central concept remains consistent: we ask these students to trust us and to do something that we know is very hard—to move out of their comfort zone and take on a genre that is a challenge to them, for whatever reason. Perhaps it's a genre that they love to read but never felt capable of writing (like Theresa's lyrics); perhaps it's a genre that's totally new to them, that they've only vaguely heard of (like microfiction); perhaps it's a genre that they've tried before but without much success (like memoir or literary analysis); or perhaps it's one that they know they need to learn how to do, but just haven't had the guts, or opportunity, to try (like Nikitha's college entrance essay).

Amazingly, over the years, most students have trusted us enough to jump into the unknown and try. In part, we think it's because we establish right away that they won't be all alone in their journey. As their teachers, we offer them strategies, skills, and tools to learn about their chosen genre through whole-class minilessons and individual conferences. As participants in a class community filled with individual researchers, we share their discoveries about their chosen genres and search for connections across genres. We also make it clear immediately that the final piece doesn't have to be the best sonnet, the best editorial, the best cover letter ever written: it just has to demonstrate what the student has learned about the genre and represent a good faith effort at that learning. We encourage students to take risks, and we let them know that we understand that their first time through a genre is probably not going to result in a masterpiece. And, finally, we try to place the unfamiliar genre unit within a semester or year of study in genre in general. In other words, by the time students get to this journey into the unknown or challenging genre, they've had plenty of experience thinking about the concept of genre and experimenting in whole-class genre studies.

And so the students begin. They figure out the genre they want to explore and they find samples of that genre. They read extensively in their genre, taking notes about what they notice, searching specifically for both similarities and inconsistencies in the examples they've chosen, and trying to identify what makes this genre a genre. They create tentative lists of qualities for their genre, imagining a definition, making sure to mention those examples that don't seem to fit and to hypothesize about why that might be so. They take that knowledge and write their own version of the genre, making sure to pick a topic that is meaningful to them. And, finally, they reflect on the experience—both in terms of how their own version of the genre measures up to the models they noticed and how their understanding of genre in general has taken shape over the course of this study.

Why do we ask them to try such a thing? And what is it about the Unfamiliar Genre Project that keeps us rethinking and revising it, fascinated by its effect on our students? Two primary principles about teaching writing form the basis of this project.

First, we believe in the importance of genre as a way to study writing. A focus on genre helps students discover how writing works in a way that reflects the reality of writing in the world at large. Writing, we all know, is not a particularly consistent concept. What is considered good writing constantly shifts and changes depending on the audience, context, purpose, and genre. In other words, what is considered good writing for song lyrics (e.g., catchiness, repeated lines and phrases, use of slang or dialect) might not be the same as what's considered good writing for a college entrance essay (e.g., organization, compelling lead, standard conventions and grammar). We've found that a focus on genre helps students see the differences that exist among these various kinds of writing and think about why they exist. And we believe that students who see the flexibility of writing and who understand the necessary shifts writers make in sentence structure, diction, kinds of examples, tone, and voice to reach particular audiences in particular ways are well prepared to take on the many kinds of writing they will face throughout their school lives and beyond.

Second, while we believe in a genre approach to writing pedagogy, we know that we can never hope to cover all the genres that exist (and that may exist in our students' futures). There just aren't enough teaching days to do that. Thus, when we ask students to explore an unfamiliar genre of their own choosing in a supportive community environment, we hope we are helping them learn the strategies they'll need to take on the new genres that will confront them in their future worlds. Teaching students *how* to learn rather than supplying them with all the content is a bedrock principle of this project.

This is a book about these two principles and how they resulted in our journey through the Unfamiliar Genre Project. We offer our thoughts as an introduction to the Unfamiliar Genre Project, situated in the contexts of our teaching, our students, and ourselves. Because we have taught the project in many different settings, we have adapted and changed it over time, depending on the class, the needs of the particular students, and our own learning curve as teachers who are constantly revising our approaches. In this book, then, we share with you our current best thinking about this project, situating these ideas in the contexts of several classes and numerous students.

This is a particular kind of book, what we think of as theorized practice. We know some readers want to get right to the "good stuff"—the examples from the kids, the how-to portions that offer the specifics of how we organized the classroom, the minilessons, and the assessment rubrics. And we promise: you'll find all of that in the chapters that follow. But we also passionately believe that the best teaching happens not just from figuring out the "how to do it" but in formulating an understanding of how specific approaches draw upon particular beliefs—in our case, beliefs about what genre is and why genre study can help students become independent and successful writers. The wonderfully articulate compositionist Ann Berthoff says this better than we possibly could:

Theory gives us perspective; just as it allows us to determine sequences, it saves us from too much particularity. Teachers have to be pragmatic; they have to be down to earth, but being down to earth without knowing the theoretical coordinates for the landscape is a good way to lose your sense of direction. We English teachers are given to recipe swapping—and that can be dangerous. In my ideal commonwealth . . . I would order the closing down of the Exercise Exchange. . . . The NCTE would not be allowed to operate it unless they instituted a Theory Exchange. And you couldn't get the recipe unless you also went there. I have a friend in the Denver schools who does just that. When her colleagues say, "Oh, that sounds wonderful! Can I have that exercise?" she says, "Sure, but you have to take the theory too." And the exercise comes typed up with a little theoretical statement at the top, an explanation of whatever aspect or function of learning the assignment is meant to exercise. That combination of theory and practice can help prevent what so often happens: . . . You hear something described that sounds good; it's obviously foolproof; you try it, and it doesn't work. So you feel terrible because this great exercise is a proved success—and you flubbed it. By reminding us that reading and writing happen in contexts . . . theory can save us from wasting time blaming ourselves or our students. (1987, 32)

With this piece of wisdom in mind, we ask that you bear with us as we begin this book with some discussion about the beliefs, principles, and theories (with a lowercase *t*) that inform our understanding of how to teach this way. Think of it as a way, as Berthoff might say, to maintain a sense of direction as we take you on our journey through the Unfamiliar Genre Project.

In Chapter 1, we talk a bit about genre and the complicated ways in which people are currently thinking about it, about the principles that underlie genre study for us, and about the ways in which the Unfamiliar Genre Project grew integrally for us out of these understandings.

In Chapter 2, we start to get more into the nitty-gritty: what we see as the basic components of a genre study approach to teaching writing and how such an approach might work in a variety of classrooms (from novel centered to writing workshop).

Chapter 3 brings you squarely into a particular high school composition classroom (which Sarah taught and in which Cathy was a participant-observer for a semester) and focuses on how we worked with these students to build a concept of genre in the classroom, sharing the specifics of some of the whole-class genre studies we use to introduce students to the idea of unfamiliar genre, especially as a way of thinking about what genre means.

Chapters 4 and 5 focus on our most recent version of the Unfamiliar Genre Project at the high school level, detailing organizational structures, specific lessons, and samples from students. In Chapter 4, we lay out these details, while in Chapter 5, we offer a complete Unfamiliar Genre Project for you to consider.

Finally, in Chapter 6, we introduce some variations on the project: short vignettes about how we've taught it in multiple settings. Sarah shares her versions of the Unfamiliar Genre Project in both a journalism class and a literature class titled Short Readings. Cathy then offers some perspective on the original Unfamiliar Genre Project as it played out in a preservice methods course at her university.

We urge you to read this book with consideration of your own context, your own students, and your own curricula in mind. We hope it provides you with new ways to think about genre, in particular about unfamiliar genres, and new insights about how to structure your own classes and curricula in ways that benefit the teaching and learning that surround you every day.

Acknowledgments

THIS BOOK EMERGES from a true collaboration: the two of us have had the great good fortune of being able to teach together, talk together, present together at conferences, and write (and rewrite) together—sometimes at restaurants and coffee shops, sometimes electronically, often at odd hours of the day or evening. This rare opportunity for intense collaboration was possible only because of a number of people in our individual and joint spheres who helped us carve out the time to think, research, and write about our work.

First, we want to recognize the support we received from our individual departments and schools: Cathy received support from both the Department of English Language and Literature and the Provost's Office at Eastern Michigan University in order to spend time in Sarah's class; Sarah received support from Huron High School in Ann Arbor, Michigan, to travel to conferences to present preliminary versions of this book. Thanks especially go to Linda Adler-Kassner, Ann Blakeslee, Becky Sipe, Doug Baker, and Bill Tucker at EMU as well as the entire English department at Huron, particularly Maryan Mastey, Lori Wojtowicz, Kip Wilson, and Carey Culbertson; Sarah's wonderful student teacher, Sarah Soebbing; Huron's athletic director, Dotty Davis; and Huron's principal, Dr. Arthur Williams, and assistant principal Jen Hein—friends and colleagues who always listened hard and cheered on our efforts. Thanks to Scott

McCloud, Jeff Kass, and manyother wonderful writers who've joined our classes over the years, and to Ron Stokes whose author blurb genre project inspired us. Special thanks also to Heidi Estrem, formerly at EMU and now at Boise State, who helped with the kernel of the idea of the Unfamiliar Genre Project in our discussions of good assignments.

For years, we've met monthly with the Eastern Michigan Writing Project's Teacher Research Group for pizza, wine, and lots of talk about our classroom-based research projects. As this book began to take shape, these incredible teachers helped us in the exact kind of support we needed at the moment: from thinking through the ideas behind the project, to responding to specific sections of the writing, to offering encouragement when the idea of a book seemed overwhelming. We thank them all: Jennifer Buehler, Carrie Melnychenko, Jennifer Walsh, Lisa Eddy, Kim Pavlock, Molly Fichtner, David Kangas, Kris Gedeon, and Val Johnson. And for those of you who don't have a research and writing support group like this, we encourage you to find one! These dedicated teachers who work all day in classrooms and then find the additional energy to pursue research questions to better their teaching are the models for what committed professionals can and should be.

And, of course, this book would never have been possible without the spirited and inspiring students we've had the pleasure to teach, at both Huron High School and Eastern Michigan University. There are far too many of them to mention by name, but we are so grateful for their willingness to try out new ways of learning and their honesty in helping us know what was successful and what wasn't. In particular, we thank all those students whose work is included in this book, especially Julia Rosenzweig, and the students in Sarah's third-hour composition class whose story is told in Chapter 3.

Many thanks as well to our team at Heinemann: to our editor Jim Strickland, who encouraged us in this work from the very start and whose enthusiasm buoyed us and to our production editor Elizabeth Valway, who helped make the book come together during the final stages.

Writing a book while being teachers, friends, daughters, wives, and moms can sometimes be a precarious balancing act. The love and support of our families and friends, their willingness to do more than their share during strategic moments in the writing, and their constant presence have helped more than they will ever know. We thank them all for their constant support; this counts exponentially for Andy, Seth, and Jesse Buchsbaum; Derek Vaughan, Ellie, Livvy, and Charlie Andrew-Vaughan.

Why a Focus on Genre?

DOESN'T IT SEEM AS IF the word *genre* crops up everywhere you turn right now? It's as if genre has taken center stage as a way to think about literacy instruction from kindergarten to college; as a focal point for a number of textbooks about English/language arts instruction; and as an increasingly vital component of local, state, and national standards documents. Here are just a few of the examples that we've come across recently:

- In her book *Writing a Life*, Katherine Bomer (2005) demonstrates how to teach memoir as a genre study, immersing students in the experience of reading and writing memoir as a six-week unit. And despite the seeming irony, she even suggests that a focus on memoir writing can be tweaked to help students prepare for standardized writing tests.

- Heather Lattimer, in her book *Thinking Through Genre* (2003), lays out a unit-by-unit plan for incorporating genre study in classrooms for grades 4–12, specifically suggesting genre study as a means of integrating reading and writing workshop.

- A variety of books written in response to Tom Romano's (2000) now classic multigenre project think through how to help students learn to work with various genres in preparation for the project. (See, for example, Melinda Putz's *A Teacher's Guide to the Multigenre Research Project* [2006].)

- Numerous college-level books and articles about writing are saturated with thoughts about how to teach through a genre-based approach. Most of these suggest that by focusing on genre, students can be better prepared to face the multiple kinds of writing they'll be asked to do in their college careers (and beyond).[1]

- In the state of Michigan (our home state), recent content standards and grade-level content expectations emphasize genre-based approaches for children as young as elementary age. For example, second graders are expected to "identify and describe the basic elements and purpose of a variety of narrative genre including poetry, fantasy, legends, and drama" (Michigan Department of Education 2006, 4).

These examples and a host of others demonstrate that educators at all levels are thinking about interesting ways of using genre in English language arts classrooms. More and more, we see genre being taught through *genre studies*, that is, a way of arranging curriculum so that at least some of the teaching is done through immersion in one or a series of genres: students read in the genre, study the genre, and ultimately write something in that genre. In some cases this might mean a onetime immersion, for example, studying a single genre for four to six weeks as part of a writing workshop curriculum. In others, it might mean moving every three to six weeks from one genre to the next: for example, memoir, then editorial, then literary analysis, and so on.

The Value of Genre Studies

What's striking about these many renditions and references to genre is not only the multiple ways genre studies are becoming situated into everyday literacy instruction but also the potential a genre study approach offers our students. Genre study is a valuable approach for many reasons.

First, genre study is *a means of truly integrating the English language arts.* Genre studies almost always tie together the study of literature and that of writing, so that students can continually connect their reading to the creation of text, learning to read like writers and write with readers in mind. Many genre studies even move beyond reading and writing to include visual and oral components (e.g., listening to poets read their work and performing poetry to the class or creating genres that integrate writing with art, such as graphic novels).

---

[1]See, for example, Herrington and Moran's *Genre Across the Curriculum* (2005), Johns' *Genre in the Classroom* (2002), and Freedman and Medway's *Learning and Teaching Genre* (1994), among others.

This kind of movement truly expands in important ways the integration of all the language arts.

Second, genre studies offer students *a way to explore the multifaceted nature of written texts.* When we were in school, the only valued kind of writing was the five-paragraph essay and the personal narrative (and eventually, by maybe eleventh grade, the literary analysis or research paper). It was hard to see any connection either among those genres (although we didn't even use that word then) or between that school writing and the "real writing" we saw in newspapers, magazines, and books. A genre study approach lets students know, first, that there are many kinds of writing in the world and, second, that there are indeed differences among those genres, especially in sentence structure, diction, organizational strategies, and kind of detail. That attention to multiple kinds of writing and rhetorical considerations is valuable for all writers, but especially for apprentice writers.

Genre studies also serve as a way for students *to explore the multiple processes that writers might use for various genres.* Most proficient writers don't have one writing process, but rather have many, depending in part on the genre in which they're composing. Think, for example, about how different your process is when you're writing a note to a friend as opposed to preparing an application for a grant through your school district. If you're anything like us, when you write that note, you probably use a pen to write a single draft, with little planning before writing. In contrast, when you write that grant application, you probably plan extensively, write multiple drafts at the computer, and edit carefully for typos and misspellings. An emphasis on genre studies can help students begin to understand that while the notion of process writing is absolutely central to the world of writers, different genres may elicit different processes.

A further value of genre studies is *to help students and teachers combat the increasing curricular demands of test writing.* A number of teachers are starting to use genre-based approaches to writing to set the genre of test writing in its rightful place: as one genre among many. When test writing is seen as just one more genre (like poetry or sports column or college entrance essay), with its own set of constraints and expectations, students can begin to separate that kind of writing from the other kinds they do. And when test writing is viewed in this way, rather than as the only kind of writing that truly counts, students (and their teachers) are able to assign it an appropriate value: important in some respects but not the only kind of writing we should do in school.

Finally, genre studies are *a way for students to see school writing as part of a lifelong endeavor.* All teachers face that ubiquitous, and fully appropriate, student question: When will I ever use this in real life? Genre study, we contend, provides a legitimate answer to that question. Students distinguish pretty easily between writing that is real and writing that is merely a school creation, used only to get the grade or serve some other school purpose. By studying various genres over time, students can begin to understand something about the nature of real writing and that learning writing from a genre-based stance will result in strategies that can help them when they face multiple genres in the real world.

So, we love that the concept of genre is everywhere these days; we see it as a great step forward in literacy instruction, one that will serve our students well. When genre studies sit at the center of an English language arts curriculum, students have the opportunity to truly expand their ways of thinking about writing in some valuable ways.

The Downside to Genre Studies

But here's our concern: while we love the concept of a genre study approach to teaching writing, we do worry about a couple of aspects of it, mostly because what we've seen of genre studies convinces us that they're not all created equal. While all genre studies have at their center some consistent characteristics (reading in the genre, thinking and talking about the genre, and writing something in the genre), some genre studies are really not that different from the old-school way of teaching writing that separates writing into a few specific modes. In this teaching approach, genres are taught as if they're simply formulas, with "fixed and immutable" structures that are easily classified into "neat and mutually exclusive categories and subcategories" (Freedman and Medway 1994, 1). When genre is taught as a decontextualized kind of writing with particular characteristics that the teacher (or curriculum planner) has identified as the most important qualities, form takes precedence over the ideas, the purpose, and the style of the writer. In some ways this corresponds to Ann Berthoff's striking muffin tin metaphor: that for too many teachers, "language is a muffin tin . . . , a kind of batter we then pour into molds" (1981, 25). Genre study can be taught in such a way that students are merely filling the muffin tins, much as they have done traditionally with a five-paragraph essay or other more formulaic approaches.

There is a long history through which Plato's and Aristotle's ideas about form morphed over time into four modes of writing: exposition, narrative, description, and persuasion. (For an excellent discussion of this history, see Herrington and Moran's "The Idea of Genre in Theory and Practice" in their edited collection *Genre Across the Curriculum* [2005].) In this way of thinking about genre, certain modes are seen as nearly unchanging entities, suggesting that writing is "an academic exercise instead of . . . a meaningful act of communication in a social context" (Kitzhaber 1990, 139).

At some point in this history, these four modes became synonymous with genres: students were asked to write an exposition paper, a narrative paper, a descriptive paper, or a persuasive paper (with the tacit understanding that you'd start with the narrative and descriptive because those were seen as the easiest). What this approach left out, of course, was an understanding that these modes are really not genres at all; persuasive writing, for example, can be found in hundreds of genres—from political cartoon to editorial to cover letter to satire. How persuasion works within each genre largely depends on the nature of the genre itself, as well as the audience and purpose of the specific piece. When you write a cover letter for a grant, in other words, you don't necessarily employ the same persuasive techniques as when you write a political cartoon. Clearly, then, there really is no adequate list of the qualities of persuasive (or narrative or descriptive or expository) writing that we can just hand over to students— although much writing instruction seemed to focus in that way.

In the 1960–70s a great "paradigm shift" occurred in how writing was taught. Maxine Hairston, author of the essential article "Winds of Change" (1982), explained this shift as one that moved writing pedagogy from a form-based approach to one that focused more on writing process, multiple purposes for writing (including personal growth and expression), and the rhetorical nature of the act of writing (i.e., that there are writers and audiences and contexts, which affect not only what a piece of writing looks like but how it is received). And while there are still vestiges of the old-school teaching of writing (text-books or curricula that focus mostly on the modes), more of us now incorporate at least some kind of process-based, workshop-based, rhetorically-based approach to writing instruction.

So, where does genre fit in? Is a focus on genre an old-school approach or a new one? We suggest it can be either, depending on how genre is understood and taught. While most genre studies are not nearly so formulaic as earlier approaches, we do worry when we see how these units are sometimes taught with a focus on the genre as no more than a prepackaged list of characteristics and qualities that students strive to include in their writing. In other words, this way of teaching seems to concentrate on a template for the genre, often prepared by the teacher (or curriculum guide) and handed out to the students at the beginning of the unit. Nowhere does that seem more prevalent than in some of the poetry units we've seen (and, we admit, that we've taught), in which students move from one form-based structure to another—a cinquain, a haiku, a sonnet—and are asked to compose one of each, with little exploration of the variations within a genre, of how genres might blur, or of how real writers play with forms in relation to a topic, purpose, audience, situation. In another variation, genre is taught merely by having students read a text and then compose a piece that sounds like that text, again with little study of the craft that underlies the genre or the process of writing in that genre. A classic example of this is that writing assignment in which students read Shakespearean sonnets and are then asked to write one of their own—a genre-by-osmosis means of teaching. We suspect that when genre is taught either by structure or osmosis, it's really no different than the traditional teaching of the modes of writing or the five-paragraph essay, or what Ann Berthoff talks about as fitting writing into a muffin tin.

Why We Find Genre Fascinating

We worry that a focus on form alone has the potential to miss the boat in terms of how exciting and potentially useful teaching by genre can be. While most genre units have shifted from the study of those traditional modes to more updated and familiar genres like mystery, sports writing, one-act play, and editorial, even this shift doesn't always change the underlying approach of how to teach these genres: neither doing enough to complicate the whole idea of genre nor exploring with students those blurred genres that are increasingly a part of our lives, such as graphic novels, performance poetry, creative nonfiction, even research papers. Think for example of the furor over memoir, brought to our attention by the controversy over James Frey's *A Million Little Pieces* (2003). His book, as you'll recall, raised a storm when it was heralded by Oprah Winfrey and others as a compelling memoir of Frey's traumatic life. When, later, it became clear that much of his book was based on fabricated events, many people felt cheated in some way; because we had boxed it into our conception of what a memoir should be, it lost its credibility and thus its power as an inspirational story. For those of us intrigued by genre, however, the controversy was a starting point for fruitful discussion, especially as a way to think about what it is that makes a memoir a memoir: Are all memoirs completely factual? What about the childhood conversations quoted in many memoirs? Are those exact replications? How could they be? What if the spirit of the memoir is true but some of the names, dates, and incidents are not so true? Is it still memoir? These conversations—which speak to the complicated essence of genre—are important not only for us as teachers and literacy buffs but also for our students as they face decisions in their own writing: How truthful must they be, for example, on the SAT Writing Test (a test that many have claimed is indifferent to facts)? What about their college entrance essay—does the same stance toward facts and truthfulness apply? (This was a discussion that became quite vibrant in one of our classes when a student who had composed a powerful yet creative response to a "meaningful moment in your life" college essay prompt exclaimed in dismay, "You mean it's gotta be true?")

Students, we've discovered, already know quite a bit about genre and, in fact, have an innate understanding of how blurred and complex genre can be (a surprise to us at first, since *genre* is a word we weren't even exposed to until college literature classes, when our professors usually referred to it in almost magical terms, pronounced with a slight French accent). The students we have worked with know about genre especially from their experiences with music (as listeners and writers), and they know a lot about how genres shift and change, how the musician has a distinct role in the creation of genre, and how those blurred genres of music are a large part of what makes genre such an unstable and exciting thing to talk about.

Our students' experiences with genre show us what sometimes seems missing in many classroom approaches to genre: genre as a dynamic (not static) means of communication in which students participate just by being present. Here's what we mean by this (and our thinking has been helped a lot by a number of scholars in composition studies who think deeply about these issues[2]): genre does have a lot to do with traditional ways of thinking about writing, about form and structure that help identify one piece of writing as distinct from another. Think about the genres of menu versus newspaper, of recipe versus medical form. There clearly *are* certain qualities that help create these forms; these generic characteristics help readers understand immediately what they are about to encounter and are integral to the reading process. We know what to expect, for example, when we pick up a menu, so we read it in a certain way (picking and choosing what we read; perhaps looking at the price list first or ignoring all the dishes that have meat in them; skipping to the back where we'll find the desserts); we know when we then pick up an epic poem to expect a different kind of read (perhaps we'll need several rereadings, slow readings, perhaps linearly the first time but then more recursively as we circle back to understand previous lines). If our primary understanding of genre is based on these formulaic expectations and differences, we might logically structure a classroom experience in which teachers move from genre to genre, immersing students in the experience of each genre (from reading lots in the genre to lessons about the rules and characteristics of that genre to writing their own version of the genre) before moving on to the next. Both of us have taught genre in this way, and we'd be the first to admit that this structure has worked very well with a number of students and achieves some of the goals of genre study laid out earlier.

However, we've come to realize the limits of this approach to genre study. Think for a moment back to the menu example and recall some of the menus you've encountered: from the neighborhood pub that you collapse at on a

---

[2]See, for example, the work of Bakhtin (1986), Bazerman (1997), Freedman and Medway (1994), Miller (1984), and Russell (1997).

Friday night after school to the fancy restaurant you dress up to go to on your anniversary. It's pretty clear that the genre of menu is not a static entity; in fact, it changes depending on the context of the restaurant. If you're in a family restaurant, for example, the menu may have pictures of many of the items; if you're in a fancier restaurant, the desserts may not even appear on the regular menu, but may be in a separate one, handed out after you've finished your entrée. In some restaurants the dish is given a familiar name with no explanation; in others a lengthy explanation follows, complete with information about the ingredients, how the chef prepares it, and even adjectives that describe the eating experience. The way this piece of writing is structured, in other words, has a lot to do with the audience the menu writers perceive as coming to the restaurant (Kids or adults? Food junkies concerned with all the ingredients or those searching for something that just looks good?); the situation they envision their restaurant attracting (A couple on a date who want to spend hours on dinner or a person who wants to eat and get on to the next event?). It also has a lot to do with how the restaurant wants to represent itself and by implication represent its customers (As a restaurant for those with discerning tastes or as a fast-food restaurant for families?). Haven't we all had that experience of walking into a restaurant, seeing the menu, and feeling that we didn't quite belong?

Even the menu, then, is a complex genre—one that positions itself, positions its audience, and creates a specific context. When we view it in this complexity, we can see that genre is not just a template or text type (a menu is a menu is a menu); it truly is a rhetorical construct: a construction that is informed not only by form and tradition but also by the context, the intended audience, and the positioning of author, what some people call a socially constructed concept. In other words, genres aren't inert entities that exist over time; rather, they emerge and change in response to certain situations and contexts.

Genre, in this way of thinking, is not just a template into which a writer fits her thoughts, but rather something that may begin with a template but that is further constructed by the writer, the situation, the moment. In other words, it's about the template, but not the template alone. Genres, then, have the potential to change and grow because they are dynamic in nature. Think for a moment about what this expanded concept of genre might mean in an English language arts classroom. If genres are more than text types alone, if genres are always rhetorically based, perhaps teachers need to rethink what we do when we ask our students to write a mystery, a short story, a literary analysis. This notion raises questions (which we attempt to answer in this book): Are there effective ways to make these genres more than templates in order to have our students' work reflect the complexity of the idea of genre? Is there more that we should do than provide our students with a list of qualities that we decide characterize the genre? How might we keep the teaching of genre manageable yet true to the idea that genres are dynamic and changing, that they have so much to do with audience, purpose, and positioning?

Another concern we have about some approaches to genre study has to do with the very nature of a genre study–based curriculum. As we planned and taught the course we mention throughout this book, our first tendency was to try to "cover" every genre we thought might be important in our students' lives, as if only by our covering it would students really understand a genre. We quickly discovered that not only is this approach impossible (How can you ever decide what's most important? How can you ever devote enough time to each?), but the very concept that underlies it is a bit faulty. The value of a genre study approach is not to expose students to every genre they'll ever encounter or even to provide students with "answers" to what each genre is, its qualities and characteristics neatly captured in a list. Rather, the real value of genre study is teaching students about writing in a way that they can take with them beyond the confines of our classrooms. Genre study should be, in fact, a kind of generic look at how to approach any type of writing. In other words, it is less important that students know specific strategies for writing an editorial than it is that they know how to immerse themselves in a genre like editorial, discovering (with guidance) how it is unique and how it can be written to be most effective for various readers—so that they can take those strategies for discovery and use them in their exploration of other genres, other situations, other contexts.

Randy Bomer (2003), in the foreword to Heather Lattimer's fine book *Thinking Through Genre*, expands this idea even further: "We cannot prepare students for all the genres that will be of use in their literate lives. It is laughable at this point to talk about 'the genres they need to know,' since those genres, very likely, have not been invented yet" (xi). Clearly, just giving students unit after unit of genres without doing something more—without looking at how such genres integrate, without considering their rhetorical nature, without helping students see how genre studies can help them explore genre on their own—won't really help students truly understand writing in the generic sense that seems increasingly important in teaching students for an age we can only imagine.

Given All That Complexity, What Can We Do?

What is that "something more" that we can do to better prepare students for the multiple genres with which they will be faced in their lives as writers? What can we do to honor the complexity of genre yet still make it possible to teach within the confines of a classroom setting? We have found one answer in the Unfamiliar Genre Project (UGP). Simply, the UGP gives students the opportunity to explore a genre that they find uncomfortable for some reason (perhaps because it's challenging to them or just plain unfamiliar); to use the tools of genre study we have taught them throughout the course in order to write in that genre; and to put on their metacognitive glasses while they do the project in order to reflect on their learning. This project, when situated within workshop classrooms that emphasize genre-based approaches to reading and writing instruction, asks both teacher and student to see genre in the complexity that we have talked about here: as a rhetorical construct, as a dynamic way of thinking, as more than a list of rules and regulations. And as we've both taught this project in multiple settings for several years, we have seen students think about writing and expand their writing repertoires in some amazing ways.

The roots of the Unfamiliar Genre Project come from a writing class that Cathy regularly teaches for undergraduate preservice teachers. The class, titled Writing for Writing Teachers, is modeled in many ways on the National Writing Project approach to professional development in writing, asking the preservice teachers to think hard about their own experiences as writers even as they learn new strategies and techniques for teaching writing. Over the years as these undergraduate English majors and minors have reflected on their experiences by writing and sharing stories about their own writing histories, they've learned a lot about the various reasons they and their classmates write, the processes they use, the ways writing has been meaningful (and sometimes not so meaningful) in their own elementary and secondary experiences, the role of writing outside school settings, and much, much more—all good insights that help them think about how they might teach writing in the not-so-distant future. However, the students almost always come up with this additional insight: most of them rarely struggled with writing (or if they did, the struggle usually led to some success story: they persevered and they learned; a wonderful teacher took them under wing and they learned; a teacher just didn't understand what they were getting at, and the teacher was eventually proved wrong; and on and on). The backstory for most of them is that they like writing and they think of themselves—with few exceptions—as pretty good writers. (And, in fact, most of them are quite good.) They chose English as their major or minor because they love reading and writing. So, they rightly ask, how will this immersion in their own experiences as writers help them when they face students who are unlike them, who struggle with writing in ways they never have?

The origins of the Unfamiliar Genre Project came out of this challenge: How could these preservice teachers better understand their future students, especially those students who don't see themselves as writers, who cringe every time they get a paper assignment, who procrastinate when faced with doing a writing assignment because they just don't know how? Could we create a situation for these future teachers in which they were forced to struggle a bit, forced to step back and really think about how they would figure out a way to write when they weren't confident about the writing?

This was the start of the Unfamiliar Genre Project. Cathy thought that perhaps by writing in a genre that wasn't so comfortable for them and thinking carefully along the way about what they did to be successful with that genre, her preservice teachers would learn a lot about writing. But knowing that the uncomfortable genre for each student might be different, she created an assignment in which each student would select his own genre and do an independent study project in that genre. The students in this college class spend time selecting a genre that they truly and honestly find difficult or always wanted to try but were scared to or just hate for some reason (with lots of assurances that, yes, they really are to select a genre that's hard for them and that their grade won't plummet if their final draft of that genre is less than great). They then seek multiple examples of the genre to study books in the library, articles on the Internet, stories or poems from roommates and friends—immersing themselves in reading in that genre. As they read, they reflect on what they notice about the genre, both the qualities that seem to link the examples and those that seem to shift across examples of the same genre. Eventually, they write both a piece (or a part of a piece, depending on the scope) in that genre and a reflection about their experiences with the process.

Over the years, these preservice teachers have experienced various levels of frustration and insight: some abandoning genres; some vowing to never, ever make their students write a sonnet; some discovering what really makes writing a haiku more than a simple task of counting syllables; some finding the joy in selecting just the right word to keep a microfiction within a specific word count. We also have learned that this project is not only a striking way for preservice teachers to think about struggling student writers as they themselves struggle, but additionally a hands-on entry into learning about the power of genre immersion and genre study as a means of helping writers grow. All of the college students conclude after their immersion that they will never look at any genre of writing in the same way; the balance between the constraints of writing in a genre and the strategies for making that genre sing has become a constant topic of discussion and one that these students now see as part of their repertoire of teaching. Further, these preservice teachers often amaze themselves when they realize that a once challenging genre has, with immersion and careful inquiry, become their new favorite. (See Chapter 6 for more specifics on this project at the college level, including the handout these students receive about the project.)

Sarah, as she was teaching a section of this course at the university for the first time, was intrigued by Cathy's early iterations of the project and decided to take it on not only with the college class but in her own secondary teaching—for reasons related but different.

Prior to teaching a section of Writing for Writing Teachers at the university, Sarah had employed Tom Romano's (2000) multigenre project as the culminating activity for some of her high school classes. While she enjoyed the results of this creative and thoughtful project, she found that during the final weeks of school devoted to the multigenre project, she was stretched too thin: per the assignment, every student was writing in multiple genres, many of which her students had never attempted before. As a result, most students were coming to Sarah with multiple requests for help with myriad genres. The genre minilessons Sarah created in response to these requests were becoming much larger than minilessons and, Sarah was keenly aware, felt too much like the prescriptive lists of genre characteristics she was trying to get away from. In preparation for her minilessons, she was reading examples in the genre, inquiring into the writers' craft, noticing ways in which lessons she'd taught earlier in the year transferred to these genres. But her students were getting only the results of *her* preparation; they weren't learning the skills she was employing.

Meanwhile, as she worked with the college students on their Unfamiliar Genre Projects, it quickly became clear to Sarah that the skills the preservice teachers were using to learn about their unfamiliar genres were precisely the skills her high school students needed to answer their own questions about the new and untried genres they wanted to include in the multigenre projects. The lightbulb went on: whereas the college students were engaging in a scenario in which they might struggle with a genre to better understand the experiences of their future students, the already-struggling high school students needed to learn these same skills and ways of thinking to overcome their unfamiliarity. Sarah saw how the UGP could make the connection for her high school students: it would become an intercessor that followed reading-writing workshops in which students explored their familiar genres and preceded the multigenre projects.

And that is exactly what Sarah did: that very same year, she inserted the Unfamiliar Genre Project into her English 9 curriculum so that it followed an extended reading-writing workshop and preceded the multigenre project. The results were as good as she had hoped: as with the preservice teachers, unfamiliar and challenging genres often became new favorites and students learned specific ways to approach new genres. What's more, Sarah was on maternity leave while her students finished the year with their multigenre projects; without her there, Sarah's substitute, a recently retired Spanish teacher, noted that the ninth graders transferred the skills they picked up while doing their UGPs to produce multigenre projects that painlessly included new and unfamiliar genres.

Since that first group of ninth graders, Sarah has used the project in composition, journalism, and and creative writing classes as well as literature-based courses, including English 9, American Literature, Accelerated English, Modern Readings, and Short Readings.

Why the Unfamiliar Genre Project?

The UGP is more than just a cool assignment. Our experiences with using it in different settings for different ages and kinds of students (and the reports we've gotten back from other teachers who have tried it in other settings) have convinced us that this project crystallizes for students the essence of genre study: what it can mean for them as current writers who are concerned about school writing tasks and as future writers who are concerned about making sense of their lives, making sense of the world around them, and finding ways to have their voices count in the world. Specifically, the Unfamiliar Genre Project has given our students a new understanding of and appreciation for the complexity and beauty of the act of writing. Among the understandings they've gained:

- *Each of us has genres that, for whatever reason, are easier for us to write in—and, conversely, we all have genres that are uncomfortable.* Many students (and adults) believe that you're either a good writer or a bad writer. You've heard it, too: "Oh, I'm terrible at writing, but I'm really good at math." We've heard remarks like this time and time again—in our classrooms when we assign a paper or project or from an adult at a party when we reveal that we're writing teachers. This project begins to destroy the stereotype of the gifted writer versus the untalented writer—and the idea that such a designation is unchangeable. Together we discover the reasons some students are drawn more naturally to particular genres, perhaps because they love reading in those genres or they've had experience in those genres or they are just more comfortable thinking in a particular way (e.g., narratively versus analytically). But we also discover quickly that even those writers perceived by the class as the "good" writers have some genres that make them uncomfortable, too. Talent in writing and comfort in writing, it becomes clear, are not necessarily consistent across genres. Recognizing this fact, celebrating this fact, making this fact a part of the history of a writing class, helps all students gain more confidence as writers and invites those students who might otherwise think of themselves as nonwriters to join the community of writers. If even Joseph, the most "talented" writer in the class, struggles with some kinds of writing, maybe Rebecca's struggle with opinion columns doesn't mean she's a bad writer. And when Joseph seeks help in writing a song from Rebecca, who has shown her talent in that area, the classroom makes great gains in truly becoming a community of writers.

- *Strategies exist for learning new genres and making them your own.* If students learn how to approach a new genre in a supportive school setting, one that includes inquiry, immersion, and instruction (concepts we introduce and explore in the next chapter), they will learn more than just how to write in that one genre. They will learn a process that will help them when they face the multiple genres in life that never show up in school. In other words, students learn that there are ways to investigate and uncover the secrets of writing, and once they learn to demystify writing, they gain great skill and confidence in their ability to do so again. Once they know they can figure out how to write in an unfamiliar genre, they will have a model for how to do this when, in their future, they face a kind of writing that is new or uncomfortable.

- *While genres have particular constraints and demands that make them unique, there are also ways of writing that cross genres.* While most genre studies stress the uniqueness of particular genres, a project like this also demonstrates that there are certain elements and processes of writing that cross borders (what we call integration, a concept we discuss more in the next chapter). In other words, the lessons they have learned about writing for certain genres (or even the innate knowledge they hold about the genres that are more familiar to them) may indeed transfer to a new genre. As students explore their individual genres in a supportive classroom setting, they begin to identify what those elements are that might define good writing generally.

- *Genres are dynamic structures that don't necessarily conform to a list of qualities.* When we teachers do all the work of teaching genre (gathering samples of the genre, assigning readings, teaching specific lessons we associate with the genre), we often keep to the examples of genre that prove the point we want to make: movie reviews are like this, sports writing is like this, mysteries must have these elements to be successful. And while we still believe it's important to have some genre studies situated in the commonalities of a genre, we recognize that what makes genre so interesting is often those outlier examples: the college entrance essays that don't conform to expectations, the scientific essay written in first person, the standardized test response that incorporates memoir. When students gather their own resources (with our help) to analyze their genre, they have to make sense of the differences that exist within the samples they've found of the genre, and they often do so in terms of each piece's rhetorical considerations: the audience, the situation, the purpose. Never have we seen students so aware of these elements as when they begin to compose their own examples of the genre they've studied.

- *Thinking about your process as a writer can help you in future writing.* We ask students to keep a journal about their journey through the project: why they chose a particular genre for this project, what has been their previous experience with this genre, what they are noticing in the samples they find, what are the difficulties and joys in studying that genre, what have they learned about the genre, what questions they still have, and so on. We all know that this kind of metacognitive thinking is good for students: because there is no way we can cover all curriculum or all knowledge, having students think carefully about how they learn and why they learn in that way can help them as they continue in their lives as thinking adults. And we have found this particular project to be a perfect metacognitive moment. Because students are taking on something unfamiliar, they have plenty to write and reflect on, and the new knowledge they gain through this reflection seems to indicate their growing understanding of writing.

Getting Started

In Chapters 4 and 5 we describe the Unfamiliar Genre Project at a high school setting in detail. In the next two chapters, though, we talk about the prep work that goes into getting students ready to take on the project: what we mean by a genre study, the strategies that are integral to a successful genre study, and a few whole-class genre studies that have worked for us as ways to immerse students in this form of teaching and learning.

chapter 2

What Is Genre Study?

HERE'S THE QUESTION that has fascinated us for years—and that eventually led us to develop the Unfamiliar Genre Project: *How can teachers best help apprentice writers enter new genres?* In our careers, we've seen students become baffled, alarmed, and sometimes even downright surly when we've asked them to stretch their writing wings beyond the genres that feel familiar and comfortable to them. Realizing how vital it is for students to be able to compose in multiple genres, to move outside their comfort zones, we wanted to know what we could do to help them gain confidence in as many genres as possible.

In our search for answers, we thought back to some of the pioneering methodology in the field of composition studies in the 1960s. Researchers at that time, unsatisfied with many of the traditional ways of teaching writing, began to ask this deceptively simple question: How do experienced adult writers compose? That question led researchers to talk to writers, and what they discovered created a revolution that truly has transformed the teaching of writing: the notion that writing is a process; that writers go through certain stages when they compose; that prewriting, drafting, and revising are a regular part of the work of writers; that writers need time, choice, and response in order to be successful.

And so, we took a page from the work of these researchers. Just as they looked to competent adult writers to find answers to their question, we wanted to consider how actual, everyday experienced writers enter a *new* genre. What do they do when faced with writing in a genre they haven't experienced? What resources do they seek in order to make sense of the genre?

Randy Bomer, in his foreword to Heather Lattimer's book *Thinking Through Genre*, gave us some beginning insight as he explained how he went about writing a foreword when he had never written one before:

> For a while, I floundered around with it, trying to figure out the nature of the task. Finally, I got up and went to my bookshelves and pulled down a few books with forewords. I read them, with questions in mind: What kind of thing is this? How does it go? When it seems to work, what are the smaller elements making it work? These questions helped me find a length, a structure (or range of structures), a voice, and a relationship to other texts (especially the rest of the book). A sense of genre helped me get started, helped me know how to go forward through the sections of a text, and helped me craft an ending. It let me organize my energy, my attention, and the content of my thoughts. (2003, ix)

Thinking, as Bomer did, about what any of us do as we enter a new genre is an intriguing stretch for teachers before we start teaching genre. We encourage you to try it: think about a time when you had to write in a genre that was new or less comfortable for you. How did you do it? What was your process like? Here's what we discovered when we answered this question ourselves:

Cathy: A couple of years ago at the annual NCTE convention, I was suddenly thrust into a genre in which I had little experience: the introduction. I was asked to introduce three different people at three occasions for the conference: a keynote speaker for a large session, the recipient of an award at another session, and an author who was speaking at a luncheon. While I had not written many introductions before, I certainly had heard a lot, and so I had a wealth of material to draw upon, especially the introductions I had heard others give at this same conference over many years of attending. So, I started by trying to recall these other introductions I had heard and determining what they had in common: how long they were, how specific they were, what kinds of information seemed to be standard practice. I also thought a lot about what I liked and didn't like about the introductions I had heard: I most liked the ones that gave more than a list of honors and awards, that seemed to be more than just a repeat of the speaker's resume; I also didn't like the ones that started to be more about the introducer than the introducee! I liked the ones that seemed to have a memorable anecdote about the person, that made the person come to life. I then thought about what I knew about public speaking, especially in terms of writer's craft: I knew that audiences had difficulty following the long, multiclause sentences I tend to write; I knew that the transitions had to be crystal clear; and I knew that I would have to emphasize with my voice certain words and phrases. Finally, I started thinking about the information that I would want to include. I went to websites about the people I would be introducing, I gathered resumes, and, for the one speaker I knew well, I thought about stories I knew about her. At a certain point, I realized that these three introductions, because they were for different kinds of events, would not really look alike. One, for example, was to introduce an author whose books I had read but whom I didn't know, an author who I realized would be familiar to probably half of the audience, but a stranger to the other half. That was really different from the introduction I would write for the outgoing president of NCTE, a friend and mentor who had literally changed my life and who—at least by name—was well known to all those who'd be attending.

Sarah: An unfamiliar—and intimidating—genre I took up directly after my first turn at teaching the Unfamiliar Genre Project to high school students was a journal article about my experience with the project. I knew when I read a call for articles in *English Journal* that focused on research in the classroom that this was the perfect subject, but I'd thought that many times before and had never taken the plunge into actually attempting to write an article. This time was different, though, because I thought there was no better test of the Unfamiliar Genre Project than to write an article about it using the lessons I had learned. I started with what I knew about this genre of journal article: that I'm always hooked by articles that begin in the classroom, that I don't finish reading articles that aren't practical or useful, that I respect writers who can balance clarity and voice. I had an idea for my lead—the opening lesson for the project—and with that, I jumped right into the writing. I suddenly had a confidence I hadn't had before: I could do this. But that was only the lead. It was time to read. And in my usual, overzealous way, I read and reread a lot of articles. I looked back at some of my favorite *English Journal* articles, found a back issue in my collection that also focused on research and read every page, walked to the mailbox, found a new issue waiting for me and devoured it. I was reading like a writer in a way I never had before: I was making mental notes of how each article was written as well as the ways it fit within and expanded the genre. I got a lot of ideas, kind of wrote the article in my head, and then sat at the computer while it poured out of me, gaps and all. By the time I sent the draft to Cathy and asked for the instruction I needed, we didn't have much time before the deadline. She gave me some great revision ideas and added her own sections that related to her part of the story. We passed the article back and forth a couple of times in the next few days, and I sent it off, feeling proud and accomplished, whether it would ever hit the pages of *English Journal* or not.

Learning how to write in a genre, we discovered, has a lot to do with understanding how the genre works from the inside out—a kind of immersion into its essence. We noticed we each started this immersion by studying examples of the genre: both those that seemed exemplary for some reason and those that seemed less successful. Cathy, for example, thought back to the many introductions she had heard; Sarah went to her stash of back issues of *English Journal*. But just studying those genres with thoughts of imitating them (or not imitating them) wasn't enough, since, as we came to realize, each time we used a genre, we were entering a new rhetorical situation. Cathy, for example, was very conscious of the difference in an introduction for an author whose name and work were familiar to the audience and one for an unfamiliar author; Sarah was answering a call for manuscripts and imagined her writing project colleagues (and herself) as her audience. We could immediately see that tied into the notion of immersion in a genre was thinking about the rhetorical situation of this particular moment of writing: Who is the audience? What are the audience's expectations and needs? Who are you as a speaker or writer? How are you constructing yourself (as apprentice, as expert, as awestruck groupie)? How do you want others to see you? What is the situation? How does this writing meet the needs of that experience?

Introducing Students to the Concept of Genre

So how might this thinking about our own entry into new genres help us (and you) introduce adolescent writers to the concept of genre? The intent (and inherent challenge) of genre study in school becomes how to take these individual experiences of exploring and learning new genres and re-create them in a class of thirty adolescent writers—no easy task, to be sure, when you have students with different levels of experience as writers, different familiarity with genres, and different inclinations toward particular kinds of writing. Still, as we have worked over the last few years with genre pedagogy, we've come to recognize four elements that are vital to successful genre study, which we call the four *Is*: immersion, inquiry, instruction, and integration.

Immersion

Simply put, the best way to learn about a genre is to immerse yourself in it. In a classroom genre study, that means surrounding the students with examples of the genre under consideration. At the most basic level, students should read examples of the genre to get a sense of its structure, that is, to see what it is that makes a mystery a mystery or a sports story a sports story. Beyond that, though, we want students to immerse themselves in a genre by reading in a purposeful and deliberate way. In order for students to move beyond the surface level of genre, in order to understand more deeply how a genre works, we want them to *read as writers* who are curious about how others have done what they are about to do (or are doing). We want them to read behind the words to discover the craft that brought the words to the page. We want them to evaluate the writing to understand both the self-conscious and the unconscious choices the writer made as she wrote, the rhetorical context the author was writing for, as well as the impact the writing has on our own rhetorical context.

In order to make that truly happen, we must expose students to multiple examples of the genre under consideration; this multiplicity speaks to the first quality of what we mean by immersion. Too often, we've seen genre studies presented as study of a single model text, the text that students are asked to read, discuss, and imitate. While this approach provides a certain degree of depth, it also has important limitations: when students have the opportunity to look only at a single text, they lose the chance to consider how dynamic a genre is and how each rhetorical situation helps create the text. In other words, instead of really studying the genre with its multiple variations, they are just imitating a single example. By simply adding multiple samples, we open up opportunities for comparison, and, with each additional sample, the possibilities compound.

What we also mean by immersion is this: studying all kinds of texts and not just written examples. Think, for example, about the genre of introduction mentioned earlier. One way to learn about that genre would be to listen to introductions on the radio or watch introductions on television. Similarly, we can expand our immersion into poetry or drama by listening to or watching those genres in action. Our vision of immersion has students literally surrounded by the genre: examples of texts they can read (even covering the walls), audio that they can listen to as a class or in small groups, DVDs on a computer or projector that they can again study singly or together, choral readings by the class members, and so forth. When immersion is truly working, our classroom should be, as our friend (and middle school teacher extraordinaire) Kathleen Hayes Parvin describes it, "dripping with literacy."

Inquiry

Immersion is a great start, but simply surrounding ourselves with all those texts is not enough. The essence of genre study is inquiry into that genre: as our students immerse themselves in the genre under consideration, we want them to ask multiple and deliberate questions about the genre, questions we hope they'll remember when they begin writing their own pieces. While we are reading (and listening and viewing), then, we encourage students to ask specific questions about authors' choices as well as the larger constructs that surround those choices: the genre itself, the rhetorical contexts of our and others' work, the roles we assume as readers and writers. In part the questioning is designed so that students will start to make sense of what makes this genre hold together, but in part it functions as a way to get toward the dynamic nature of the genre. So questions might range from What characteristics do these examples have in common? to Why is this example written in first person when the other examples are written in third? What kinds of sentence structures seem predominant in most of the samples? What does that tell you about what the writer of this piece is trying to accomplish? What does it help you learn about the genre?

Why is this concept of inquiry so important for our students? When any learner is integrally involved in the process of discovery (rather than just being spoon-fed information), the learning is so much more meaningful. Our challenge as teachers is to provide an environment for students to discover how to make visible what has seemed invisible so that they might go on to make their own discoveries. The end goal is not to fill them with facts, but to teach them how to learn.

How do we make that kind of inquiry happen in a genre study? To begin, it happens naturally as we model our own questions about texts and about genres. Often when we study a genre in which we're not well versed, the questions arise out of true curiosity. One of the genre studies that we'll show you in this book is a good example—that of comics. We had the rare opportunity to bring Scott McCloud, a well-known comic book artist and author of *Understanding Comics* (1993), into one of Sarah's classes for two days (an experience we talk about more in Chapter 3). Given that opportunity, we believed studying the genre of comics would be appropriate, although a little scary as neither of us knew a lot about it. But as we read his book, as we drew upon the students' knowledge of comics, and as we looked more carefully at a range of comics, from *Maus* (Spiegelman 1986) to the Sunday comics in our local newspaper, we developed a number of questions to which we truly didn't know the answers. And the kids responded in kind by genuinely raising their own great questions for us, for each other, and for Scott. What, we wondered together, is the difference between a graphic novel and a comic? What does the frame have to do with the structure of a story? How do you show a character is thinking? Is talking? How do you decide on a number of frames? In other words, our own genuine questions about the genre modeled for students a way of approaching this kind of study. This same questioning mind-set can come through in almost any genre study, especially if we, as teachers, really open up our minds to be inquirers ourselves and not only providers of answers.

Instruction

Sometimes, of course, a teacher's job *is* to have some answers, especially when it comes to helping students learn strategies for reading and writing. We've found that genre study is the perfect venue for the kind of situated instruction that is typical of reading and writing workshops: instruction in process, craft, conventions, or classroom structure, usually in the form of minilessons. By minilessons, we have in mind what Nancie Atwell, Lucy Calkins, and others have described as (usually) short, focused lessons about a topic that connects directly to the students' writing. Teachers choose the topic for the lesson, create a plan that explains the topic in a hands-on fashion, and ask the students (as much as possible) to apply the lesson to the writing they are doing.

All of us who use minilessons in a workshop setting know one of the major challenges of this approach: how to make the lessons apply immediately to all students all the time. This is a particular issue when the workshop is one truly driven by student choice, where some students might be working on memoir, others on poetry, and others on editorials. How can you find the right minilesson that will apply to all those genres, all those writers' immediate needs? Most of us find ways to work around this challenge, by having students record the gist of these lessons—in their own writer's notebooks or in class sheets we keep in a binder—so that even if the lesson doesn't apply directly to the writing they are in the midst of that day, they can look back at the lesson at a future time. But we've found that even the most well-organized version of this solution sometimes still leaves kids floundering.

One of the delights of genre study is that these lessons generally do apply to both student needs and the genre under consideration. While some more generic minilessons can fit in at almost any point of a genre study (e.g., lessons on how to set up your writer's notebook or how to have a peer conference), others arise naturally from the particular genre. For example, we may teach students to write thought shots à la Barry Lane in a memoir unit, conduct a minilesson on transitions or theses in a standardized test writing unit, or deliver a short lesson on quotation marks in a literary analysis unit—focused minilessons connected to the genre under study. Still other minilessons arise from the specific needs of the students at that point in the class. If it becomes clear that students are struggling with leads, naturally we'll create a minilesson about leads at that moment. What is interesting about genre study, of course, is that we may come back to the notion of leads again and again over the semester, as we think together about how leads might vary, depending on the genre: a lead for a memoir, for example, would be quite different from a lead for a news story. Returning to the technique deepens our understanding of it—and the opportunity to think across genres.

Integration

The notion of thinking across genres is the essence of the last characteristic of successful genre studies: integration. While it is important for students to understand how genres differ, it's also important for them to understand how certain aspects of good writing and certain qualities of good writers transfer across genres. Think of a Venn diagram in which two distinct genres do not stand separately, but in some ways overlap. For example, while the genres of feature articles and poetry are pretty distinct, feature article writers often draw upon the literary devices commonly employed in poetry, providing some transfer across the genres. This essentially is what we mean by integration. A vital aspect of genre study, then, is to help students recognize what the genres they are studying have in common. Otherwise, it may seem that the purpose of genre study is merely extensive coverage of every genre that exists, a concept we know is both erroneous and impossible. Students need to see that while we might cover only a limited number of genres in a class, the important lesson here is to learn both the strategies for learning about a new genre and the overall understandings of writing that emerge from close scrutiny of a few particular kinds of writing.

In other words, we think of integration as the way to step back and think about what cuts across all writing, the big picture of genre study. While we recognize that a menu is not a literary analysis, and a sports story is not an editorial, we also know that all these genres do share certain characteristics of good writing. Further, it's important for students to see that we don't start from scratch each time we enter a new genre; of course we call on our prior knowledge and experiences, which goes a long way toward demystifying the unfamiliar. Once you are comfortable writing in certain genres, you can take the knowledge, strategies, and skills from those genres and apply them in a new setting. Students, we believe, benefit greatly from seeing these connections among genres.

One way to promote this kind of integration is to continually reference the basic qualities the students have discovered about the genres they've studied over the semester. Sarah, for example, has used an adaptation of Spandel's Six Plus One Traits of Analytic Writing as a generic rubric for the entire course, with students filling in specifics for each of the traits about a particular genre during each unit (Spandel 2001). In other words, she introduces in early minilessons the rubric with its broad-based traits: ideas and content, organization, voice, word choice, sentence fluency, presentation, and proofreading considerations. As she then immerses students in the first genre study of the year, she asks them to help her define what those traits look like for that genre: What does content typically look like in this genre, how is this genre organized, what is vital about voice here? Students then define the characteristics of the trait on their rubric chart. As the semester progresses and students have multiple rubrics based on the same seven traits but defined in some similar and some different ways, they have a graphic depiction of the similarities and differences among the genres. This depiction allows for the kind of integration that is vital to a genre study (i.e., *all* writing should be concerned with ideas and content, organization, voice, word choice, sentence fluency, presentation and proofreading; however, how those qualities show themselves might differ from genre to genre). (See Chapter 3 for an example of how the author blurb genre study rubric builds upon the more generic one developed by Spandel.)

Another way to promote this kind of integration is an exercise Sarah did with a class we talk about extensively in this book, a composition class filled with a number of struggling writers. Four weeks into the class, as she handed out individual interim grade sheets designed to let students know where they currently stood, Sarah anticipated that some students would be disappointed in their grades. She set up this lesson both as a way to let them process their response to these marks and as a way to make more immediate the ideas about genre and rhetorical situation that we'd been discussing in class. She began by asking them to write a journal entry to themselves about their grade: "Are you happy with this grade? Are you sad?" After they wrote for a few minutes, she asked them to switch gears and write a letter to her, explaining to them that this interim grade would be sent home to their parents by the end of the week, unless they did something to change their grade in the next few days. "Now is your chance to let me know what you intend to do about this grade. Write to me." After another short writing time, Sarah asked the students to consider the two pieces of writing they'd just done and to talk about what they found to be similar and different in these pieces. Immediately, students pointed out that, although the content of the two pieces was pretty similar, variations occurred because of the differences in genre, purpose, audience, and even representation of themselves. They talked about the changes in organization (from freewriting in the journal entry to "more structured" in the letter to Ms. Andrew), in language (from "raw" in the journal to "standard" in the letter), and in their representations of themselves (from "real" in the journal to "fake" in the letter). As the discussion continued, Sarah assigned them one more related piece of writing: a letter to either their parents or a college admissions officer explaining what happened with the grade. The next day's discussion about these new writings led us to chart what happens to word choice, length, organization, voice, content, and presentation within and across these various genres.

This kind of integration is primarily important so that students can think about the connections among what might seem disparate kinds of writing. We also see its importance in a world in which blurred genres are increasingly common. It's not unusual to find writing that straddles the lines that have been traditionally established between genres: poetry that looks more like prose or creative nonfiction that blends informational writing with narration and first-person reporting.

A final aspect of integration has to do with process. Writers shift processes, we know, depending on the genre in which they're composing. As we talk about multiple genres and their similarities and differences, one interesting point of discussion for students is how our processes work within each genre. Students who claim that poetry writing, for example, requires only one draft (because, as they often tell us, "it comes directly from the heart") sometimes see that process differently when they've internalized the benefits of revision after working on a memoir (which they also insist comes from the heart, but for which revisions based on craft lessons seem much more viable). Thinking about these shifts in process and learning to be realistic about the way process works in different genres helps our students achieve one of our great goals for them: to be flexible, thoughtful composers.

How Does Genre Study Fit into a Semester of English?

As English teachers, we face an incredible number of decisions every day as we try to figure out how to best teach students to become more capable and avid readers and writers. Purposeful teachers are always thinking, rethinking, questioning, and juggling: How do I balance the requirements of my department and school, the standards of my district and state, and the beliefs I hold about teaching? Should I teach writing as a separate unit or should I integrate it throughout the semester? What are the best books to inspire my students? Should students have choice in reading or should I assign whole-class texts? And what about vocabulary, grammar, and spelling? How do I best teach those? What about David, who never seems to write when I provide in-class time? And what about Jasmine, on the other side of the room, who produces more pages of text than I can possibly keep up with?

As inquiry-based teachers, we constantly ask ourselves these kinds of questions because we know that the process of seeking answers will help us make those vital decisions about the best ways to teach reading and writing to our particular students. Sarah's evolution as a teacher of writing serves as an example of how that questioning led to changes in how she has taught. Beginning her teaching mostly steeped in novel-based instruction, she grew to incorporate a workshop structure (adapting the work of Nancie Atwell). When that approach didn't answer all the questions she had, she added another component to workshop: the multigenre paper (adapted from the work of Tom Romano). Further questions arose for her, and, as we explained previously, these led her to add more emphasis on genre study and, in particular, the Unfamiliar Genre Project.

As she has grown and changed, Sarah has not abandoned those earlier structures, but she has thoughtfully figured out ways to integrate them into a more fully developed approach to teaching. She explains that in fact she uses all of these—from novel based to workshop to genre study—with workshop becoming the structure underlying all the other approaches. Our point is this: while this book focuses in particular on genre study and the Unfamiliar Genre Project, we know that this approach relies on many others, and that all good teachers need to be thoughtful about the best way to incorporate any approaches they use for teaching writing into their own local circumstances and contexts.

That said, we don't believe that all ways of teaching writing are equal. Twenty or more years of research in composition studies—both large-scale studies and classroom-based research—have helped teachers by identifying the most effective pedagogical practices out there. A few years ago Cathy wrote about these multiple research-based approaches:

- Some teachers use a *writing workshop* approach, which emphasizes student choice in topics; time and instruction in prewriting, drafting, revising, and editing with response from teachers and peers along the way. Championed by such authors as Nancie Atwell, Linda Rief, Randy Bomer, Barry Lane, and many others, this way of teaching relies on student immersion in writing, punctuated by teacher-directed minilessons.

- Some teachers use *writing-to-learn* strategies in the English classroom, strategies that invite students to write in journals or reader response logs; to create narratives from the point of view of an author or character; to write dialogues among characters; and a host of other strategies. Gleaned from the wonderful literature on writing across the curriculum strategies, this approach invites students to study literature by writing along the way, writing to discover what they're learning about the literature as they read.

- A growing number of teachers use a *genre-based* approach, which mixes literature and writing, immersing and instructing students in one genre at a time by reading while writing in that genre: genres such as memoir, poetry, short story and analytic writing, among others. (NCTE n.d.)

Incorporating all three creates a deep and effective way of teaching writing. A teacher might, for example, begin the semester (as Sarah sometimes does in her composition classes) with a brief genre study of a short genre and then launch a writing workshop unit that introduces students to the concepts of process writing, choice, and response. Beginning there allows both teacher and students to establish certain understandings about writing and certain rituals about how writing occurs in this classroom community. Sarah uses this unit to introduce the concepts of writer's notebooks, workshop etiquette, peer and teacher conferences, revising, and so on, as a way to set the stage for the whole semester while allowing students an opportunity to discern (and enjoy) their preferences in reading and writing: to prime the pump for the rest of the course.

Sarah often then moves on to several weeks devoted to specific genre studies (such as memoir, editorial writing, or test writing—specifics we explain more fully in the next chapter), helping students situate their understanding of reading and writing within the concept of genre. Depending on the class (i.e., is it primarily a composition course, a literature course, or a combination?), Sarah might then alternate these genre studies with thematic or author-based units that draw upon the writing-to-learn strategies mentioned earlier, but that focus on literary analysis as the writing genre under examination. In other words, she might introduce some particular pieces of literature within the traditional construct of a thematic or novel-based unit (focusing on the theme of freedom, for example, or on the novel *To Kill a Mockingbird*) but tweak that traditional approach by considering the writing for that unit through the lenses of both genre study and writing workshop: the genre under discussion might be literary analysis, which students approach through a genre lens within a workshop setting. (See Figure 2.1a and b for possible setups for literature-based and composition-based courses.)

All this is prelude in some ways for the big project of the course: the Unfamiliar Genre Project, which we talk in more detail about in Chapters 4 and 5. Again, the UGP is most successful when it builds upon the multiple approaches students have been exposed to—in particular, those of writing workshop and genre study.

An important note here: we want to stress that we don't think genre study in and of itself implies a particular way to deliver instruction and that, in fact, the teaching methods we employ are varied, depending in large part on the course, the context, and the teacher's comfort level with various approaches. In other words, while we see immersion, inquiry, instruction, and integration as tools real writers habitually use to deepen their understanding of the writing they do, we believe these tools can be taught using a range of methods.

What does that mean in terms of what our classrooms look like at any given time during the semester? We think of our teaching as a balance of teacher-directed and student-directed instruction, a balance that is in fact a kind of movement across the semester and the year as we work to help students become increasingly independent.

POSSIBLE SETUP FOR A SEMESTER IN A LITERATURE COURSE	
Unit 1 (1 week)	Genre study of a short genre, such as author blurb, surveying authors in course curriculum (see Chapter 3)
Unit 2 (3 weeks)	Genre study of either short stories or poetry, pulling from the course curriculum
Unit 3 (3 weeks)	Reading-writing workshop: students learn about workshop approaches as they select a familiar or comfortable genre in which they read and write
Unit 4 (4 weeks)	Genre study (possibly literary analysis) through a thematic unit or author study
Unit 5 (4 weeks)	Another genre study (such as drama or memoir) through a book study, author study, or thematic unit
Unit 6 (5 weeks)	Unfamiliar Genre Project (see Chapter 5)

FIGURE 2.1A. *Possible Setup for a Semester in a Literature Course*

Our classes tend to begin with more teacher-directed units that set the stage to establish teacher expertise and classroom norms, then move toward more workshop-oriented approaches that guide the students toward freedom in choices and control of their own time. Finally, the Unfamiliar Genre Project gives students the opportunity to employ the skills they learned in previous units in a very student-centered way. The goal is to move students gradually from learning writing and genre study skills toward internalizing and using these skills so that when they leave the class, they'll be equipped to confidently and successfully approach writing in new genres and for new audiences, situations, and purposes.

POSSIBLE SETUP FOR A SEMESTER IN A COMPOSITION OR CREATIVE WRITING COURSE	
Unit 1 (1 week)	Introductory survey, writing artifacts and museum walk, team building
Unit 2 (1 week)	Genre study of a short genre, such as author blurb (see Chapter 3)
Unit 3 (2 weeks)	Genre study of a second short genre, such as microfiction; alternatively, this time could be used to expand the choice writing workshop (Unit 5)
Unit 4 (3 weeks)	Genre study of a third genre, such as comic books or test writing (see Chapter 3)
Unit 5 (4 weeks)	Writing workshop (choice): students follow their own interests as they learn about their writing processes
Unit 6 (4 weeks)	Unfamiliar Genre Project (see Chapter 5)
Unit 7 (5 weeks)	Multigenre research project and celebration of voices

FIGURE 2.1B. *Possible Setup for a Semester in a Composition or Creative Writing Course*

3

Building a Concept of Genre (and Unfamiliar Genre) in the Classroom

WHOLE-CLASS STUDIES

BEFORE OUR STUDENTS take on the independence of the Unfamiliar Genre Project, we want them to first begin to build a concept of genre. Most students have an intuitive sense of genre: they know the difference between a novel they read for American lit and a song they hear on the radio; they recognize differences in how they read a menu and how they read a science textbook; and they know that they text their friends differently from how they write a lab report. Part of our job, then, is to help bring this intuitive concept of genre to the surface, in other words, to make this tacit knowledge more tangible.

As we mentioned in the last chapter, one way to do this is to immerse the students in a traditional writing workshop in which teachers encourage students to choose a kind of writing that is very familiar to them. If a student feels positive about poetry, you might urge him to write a poem for his first project. If she loves science fiction, she might write a short story or a first chapter in a science fiction novel. What's important in this approach as an introduction to the Unfamiliar Genre Project (and beyond the value of a writing workshop) is that it helps students identify what they already know about genre by immersing them in familiar and comfortable writing: how a poem is different from a lab report and how they know this is so. In many ways, this approach helps students find the language to talk about their knowledge and find ways to share that knowledge across the class so the language of genre becomes the common language of your workshop.

Another approach, one we talk about in some detail in the rest of this chapter, is to immerse students in a few discrete genre studies—especially in genres that may not be so familiar to them—as a way for a whole class to think together about genre. Studying an unfamiliar genre as a class helps students begin to construct a meaningful understanding of the concept of genre while helping them learn strategies and methods for investigating genre on their own.

In this chapter we talk about three of the many genre studies that we have done with students, which came out of a class that Sarah taught and Cathy sat in on as a participant observer. We chose to write about these genre studies and this class for a couple of reasons. First, two of these three genres are a little unusual and we don't think you'll find them in many other books about genre: the genres of author blurbs and comics. We found these were particularly useful genres for students to study, for reasons we'll explain. Second, we focus on this class because, in truth, this was one of those classes for which we can say, "If this approach worked here, it can work anywhere!" While we're not completely confident that every approach we tried was always successful, the surveys, interviews, and anecdotal feedback we received from the students assure us that their understanding of genre and of writing in general was, at the end of one semester, far more complex than it was at the beginning. As teachers, we are drawn to professional books that demonstrate realistically the inner workings of a class: the occasions when not everything was perfect, the familiar moments of near chaos that somehow make it all seem more possible! And so, while we focus mostly on what worked best, we hope to do so in the context of a real live class and real live students.

In order to give you a feel for the class, let us offer some information about the class and introduce you to some of its prominent members. First off, the class is a one-semester elective course titled Composition. Often (and this was truly the case this particular semester), this course is recommended by counselors for students who struggle in writing, although a number of students who had taken classes with Sarah before were drawn to it as well because of their appreciation of her teaching style. Students ranged from sophomores to seniors, with about half the class in twelfth grade and the other half evenly divided between eleventh and tenth. Interestingly, in this particular semester, a large number of African American students were enrolled in the class. In a school in which the African American population is 18 percent, this class had two Latino students, three Caucasian students, and eighteen African American students. We mention this for a particular reason: the issue of race was a constant in this class. Within the first days of Cathy participating, observing, and taking notes in the class, one student turned to her and said, "So, you're taking notes on the black kids, huh?" Cathy assured him she was taking notes on everyone and showed him her notebook (telling him that anytime he wanted to look in her notebook, he was welcome to). At the end of the semester, Angel[1] explained why she thought that the focus on race was so prominent and ever present in the class:

> I've never had this many black kids in one of my classes before. You know what I mean? [Usually], it's just four black kids, four Asian kids, a couple of Hispanic kids and everybody else is white. When you're in a classroom like that, you don't talk about race. So many other people are uncomfortable and you're scared they're going to reject you and talk about "oh no you're wrong," cause [the ratio is] like 20–1.

We want to be clear, though, that when we talk about the many struggling students who populated this class, we are not correlating struggling students with African American students. In this class many of the African American students were not struggling writers; in addition to their successes here, they were students in AP English, in humanities, in any number of accelerated classes where they were also doing well. There were, however, both an unusual number of African American students and a large number of struggling students in this class: students for whom homework was an afterthought, who thought of second semester senior year as the time to lay back and relax, for whom writing was either a pain or a scary proposition (or sometimes both).

Michel, for example, an eighteen-year-old emancipated minor (a student who had legally declared himself independent of parents or family) who took two hours of auto mechanics in addition to this English class on his way to graduation, took three days to actually enter the classroom and sit down. Each day, he'd come to the door, explain to Sarah that he wasn't coming in, that he hated writing, and that he must be in the wrong class. Each day Sarah would patiently invite him in, tell him to try it out, and if he really didn't like it, to see his counselor later. Nick announced on a daily basis that he was hungry and

---

[1]Because we're attempting in this chapter to capture the reality of this class' dynamics, we decided, collectively with the students, not to use their real names.

asked Sarah if she would give him a treat if he did his work. Kelvin was a rapper who talked constantly of his previous life in Detroit, proclaiming often that he was "more black" than others in the class. Marie, another emancipated minor who lived with her aunt, worked twenty hours a week, always wrote thoughtful pieces, and came in day after day posing questions that took our breath away with their power and complexity. Sabrina alternated between writing lyrics (one memorable day, she sang one to us) and yelling at her classmates to "stop acting so black."

This is the context for the genre studies included in this chapter. Some days the lessons went smoothly, and some days they didn't. Sometimes the students needed prizes and treats to keep them going; sometimes the subject itself got them excited. Some days we wondered just what would happen in class that day (including when we had a guest speaker for the comic writing genre study), and some days the class hummed along smoothly. Some students turned in everything; some students turned in nearly nothing. Some students participated; some didn't. But what we did see over the course of the semester was a fuller understanding of the concept of genre, such that students took the language and ideas of genre study into their everyday talk about writing and even into their everyday talk. And when we asked them at the end of the course to tell us what they might do in the future when faced with an unfamiliar genre, they had a bagful of strategies ready: doing research into the genre, finding examples of the genre on the Internet or in the library, or trying to discover first what was familiar about the genre.

Author Blurb

Several years ago Cathy taught a summer workshop on genre study through the Eastern Michigan Writing Project, our local National Writing Project site. Focused on a genre-based approach to teaching writing, the students in the class—all teachers from elementary through high school—created genre studies as their final projects, each designed for use in their particular contexts. The range was varied, but most fell within the standard realm of what we think of when we think of genre study: a fairy tale unit for second graders, a mystery unit for fifth graders, units in nonfiction, poetry, travel writing. Ron Stokes, then a high school English teacher and now vice principal at a local middle school, surprised us all, though, with his design: a unit on author blurbs, those short, often boring summaries of authors and their lives found on the back of book covers. To be honest, everyone's first reaction was a little hesitant. We wondered, was this for real? Was Ron just trying to get out of the assignment by doing the easiest thing possible? Was *author blurb* even a real genre?

As the presentation progressed, and as the other teachers in the class thought more fully about the author blurb genre study, we all reached the same conclusion: What a smart way to introduce genre study! In fact, ten years later, dozens of teachers in southeastern Michigan have adapted Ron's study for their own use, and Cathy regularly exposes preservice teachers to it in her classes.

Ron's rendition of the author blurb builds upon the concepts of immersion, inquiry, integration, and instruction that Cathy introduced in the class and that we wrote about in the previous chapter: *immerse* the kids in reading dozens of author blurbs. (Ron actually expands this by having students listen to author introductions on television talk shows like *Oprah* and radio interviews like *Fresh Air*.) *Inquire* together with students about the qualities that cut across this genre, the reasons why these qualities exist, and the times when authors stray from these qualities. *Instruct* students through minilessons in some of the techniques and strategies key to this genre. And finally, *integrate* these lessons into their writing by asking students to write their own author blurbs. In Ron's version, the author blurb is the first unit of the year, and the students' writing goes immediately on the wall of the classroom, in time for curriculum night and parent conferences.

Why do we think introducing students to genre study through the author blurb is such a brilliant idea? Among the reasons:

1. *The author blurb is both a familiar and an unfamiliar genre.* Students are generally aware that books have author blurbs on their back covers; many students have read them, although not many have read them particularly carefully. When asked to consider this very familiar kind of writing as a genre, students realize pretty quickly what we mean by genre. Yet because they haven't thought particularly about this kind of writing (it's one of those that just exists, but who studies it carefully?), the genre is also unfamiliar to them. It offers, then, great potential for study.

2. *Author blurbs are short.* Short is especially good as a way to introduce many of the concepts of genre study. Students can immerse themselves easily and quickly into many examples of the genre, reading and thinking through six to ten of them in a single class period. Add to that the inquiry, instruction, and writing stages, and the whole study can be reasonably and thoughtfully accomplished in a week.

3. *Author blurbs are somewhat formulaic, yet often have idiosyncratic qualities.* One of the most complicated notions of genre—from our perspective—is understanding that while most genres exist because

they adhere to particular qualities, there remains much variation, especially in consideration of audience, purpose, and voice. Author blurbs are a perfect introduction to this notion. Students can see immediately the formula that seems to govern most author blurbs. Yet when we begin to look at some of the outlier ways authors represent themselves (those blurbs that stray into first person or that add edgy humor), students can start to see that even for a short and supposedly simple genre, the notions of audience, purpose, and situation can be significant.

4. *Students who write author blurbs are immediately identifying themselves as authors.* Not only can students write author blurbs fairly easily, but in the writing, they are forced to think about themselves as writers. Ron, for example, suggests that students use the titles of pieces they've written in the past (often for school) within the blurb, thus naming that school writing as a sign of authorship. Others who have adapted this unit have asked students to either identify pieces they've already written or imagine the kind of pieces they might someday write. Over the years we've seen kids who self-identify as nonwriters develop new identities for themselves as authors, as people with both a history and a future as composers of papers, books, poems, and songs. And, beginning the semester with the author blurb study allows you to learn what students identify and value as potential writing sources and genres and thus jump-start your community of writers.

An Author Blurb Genre Study

"OK, today we're going to start a new miniunit, our first genre study of the year. Now, this may not be a genre you're familiar with. Has anybody heard of an author blurb?" Confused faces look back at Sarah. "OK, let me show you one." As Sarah pulls a book off the shelf, she shows the students where the author blurb is located and then reads it aloud.

"Today we're going to start with immersion into the genre. Here's what I want you to do. Get into groups of five and read together the author blurbs on the photocopied sheets. Start to talk together about what you notice that is common across these, what is different, what you like, and what you don't like. Then we'll get back together and have a discussion."

As students gather in groups to talk about these examples, they begin to name certain qualities that they notice in common. Some characteristics jump out immediately to the students: they notice the author's name is up front, titles of previously written books are named, and specific awards and honors are listed. Other ideas seem to need fuller discussion: How many paragraphs? It seems to vary. Why do some of them have quotes? Is that something an author blurb has to have? Most of them have pictures of the authors. Does it have to include a picture to be an author blurb? Marie questions an author blurb taken from an old book by Dick Gregory in which he is identified as "a comedian, social satirist, Negro, pioneer." "How can they call him a Negro?" she asks. "Who wrote this?" We talk about language over time and how things change. Students bounce back and forth between creating a list of characteristics and realizing that those characteristics and qualities they notice can vary greatly within the genre.

Sarah brings the class together and asks the students to share their findings. As she records the groups' ideas, some groups that found unusual and interesting characteristics get oohs and aahs from their peers. As Marcus and his group name their characteristics, he stands and high-fives the other members of the group each time they get a compliment on a characteristic. Students argue about certain characteristics, questioning whether they're true for all author blurbs or why a certain characteristic makes sense in a particular example. By the end of the class period, they have collected a number of qualities, recorded by Sarah on the overhead and by them in their notebooks. Among their findings:

- Author name is the first thing mentioned.

- Font is usually bigger for author name.

- Sometimes talks about where author lives.

- The picture seems to represent who they are as people.

- Sometimes lists jobs they've held.

- Written in third person.

- Simple sentence structure.

- Written in paragraphs, usually one to three.

- Names the genres of their book.

- Lists awards, prizes, and achievements.

- Notes if the book is a *New York Times* best-seller.

- Sometimes explains why the author wrote it or an inspiration.

- Sometimes mentions author's struggles, personal stories, or background.

- Word choice: uses words like *distinguished*.

- Sometimes has a personal quote.

- Lists titles of other books author has written.

- Written in standard English.

- Sometimes names the college author went to.

As students take notes on these characteristics, Sarah explains that they should keep a running list of the qualities they notice. "Read some author blurbs at home tonight on books that you have, and add anything new you notice." Students leave class the first day with a list of qualities, some good discussion about why certain qualities might be found in particular blurbs and not others, and an assignment for the next day: to draft three versions of a lead to an author blurb about themselves.

As the rest of the week progresses, Sarah takes them through a number of invitations for reading and writing. One day, students work with Sarah to develop a rubric that reflects the most important characteristics that they have identified, melding these qualities into the Six Plus One Traits rubric developed by Vicki Spandel (2001), which several teachers use in Sarah's school. As we mentioned in Chapter 2, this exercise lets students see how the characteristics of the author blurb both fit into the overall traits of good writing and become very specific for this particular genre. (See Figure 3.1.)

On another day, students bring in drafts of their own blurbs for conferences with Sarah, Cathy, and each other, basing their conferences on the rubric that they developed. (See Figure 3.2.) Throughout the week, she also teaches minilessons on issues of craft and usage connected to the author blurb: both what Atwell (1998) calls *procedural minilessons*, like how to confer with each other, for example, and *conventions minilessons*, such as how to use complete sentences in their writing (which becomes the proofreading focus for this rubric). Throughout the week as students write and revise, we take individual digital photos of them so they can create a blurb that looks like the real thing. (See Figure 3.3 for a description of the setup for the week.)

The student author blurbs that result from this study demonstrate students' beginning understanding of writing in a genre: to a student, they fit the genre beautifully and set the stage for the more complex discussions of genre that will emerge over the semester. It's a good start! (See Figure 3.4 for sample student author blurbs.)

SIX PLUS ONE TRAITS RUBRIC					
	Shows Skill Throughout	Strengths Outweigh Weaknesses	Equal Strengths and Weaknesses	Weak, but Made an Effort	No Effort
Ideas and Content					
Organization					
Voice					
Word Choice					
Sentence Fluency					
Presentation					

Adapted from Spandel (2001).

May be copied for classroom use. © 2009 by Cathy Fleischer and Sarah Andrew-Vaughan from Writing Outside Your Comfort Zone *(Heinemann: Portsmouth, NH).*

FIGURE 3.1. *Six Plus One Traits Rubric*

AUTHOR BLURB RUBRIC BASED ON COMPOSITION STUDENTS' OBSERVATIONS					
	Shows Skill Throughout	**Strengths Outweigh Weaknesses**	**Equal Strengths and Weaknesses**	**Weak, but Made an Effort**	**No Effort**
Ideas and Content • Titles of publications • Awards, prizes, achievements, best-sellers • Background/personal story: born, education, jobs (past and current), where live, family • Quote from author • Inspiration for book • Publisher • Genres and subgenres author writes in • Photo represents author; suggests image					
Organization • Formula: name + titles and honors + personal info + family and where live • 1–3 paragraphs					

(continues)

May be copied for classroom use. © 2009 by Cathy Fleischer and Sarah Andrew-Vaughan from Writing Outside Your Comfort Zone *(Heinemann: Portsmouth, NH).*

FIGURE 3.2. *Author Blurb Rubric*

AUTHOR BLURB RUBRIC BASED ON COMPOSITION STUDENTS' OBSERVATIONS
(Continued)

	Shows Skill Throughout	Strengths Outweigh Weaknesses	Equal Strengths and Weaknesses	Weak, but Made an Effort	No Effort
Voice • Third person • Standard English • Straightforward, plain					
Word Choice • Compliments: *distinguished*, *outstanding* • Standard English					
Sentence Fluency • Simple sentences (subject + verb)					
Presentation • Photo in B&W, head shot, placed above writing • Credits photographer • Author's name in bold (font is special) • Approximately 3 inches wide					
Proofreading • Focus on complete sentences					

May be copied for classroom use. © 2009 by Cathy Fleischer and Sarah Andrew-Vaughan from Writing Outside Your Comfort Zone (Heinemann: Portsmouth, NH).

Figure 3.2. *(Continued)*

AUTHOR BLURB GENRE STUDY

The project this week is to write an author blurb about yourself. It can be real or imaginary. Tell us about yourself as a writer. Look into the future and imagine the titles of the books you'll write. Fantasize: what would you love to write and publish? The polished final draft must look and read just like the blurbs you see at the end of nearly every book on the market.

Monday we'll immerse ourselves in the genre. This means that we'll read lots of samples. When we read, we'll read like writers: we'll pay attention to the way it is written, the choices the author made, the structure and form of the genre. This is called *inquiry*; as we read, we'll keep a running list of our observations.

Monday's Homework: Bring your writer's notebook to class! Draft three versions of the first line (the lead) of your author blurb. Read the author blurbs on the books you own; add to your notes.

Tuesday we'll set up our writer's notebooks, so come prepared to organize! Once we have our notebooks set up, we'll revisit our observations and add any you came up with last night. We'll have a miniworkshop today to confer about our leads.

Tuesday's Homework: Draft your author blurb. Continue to read every blurb you can find.

Wednesday's lesson will be to create the rubric we'll use to grade our final blurbs. Then, to test our rubric, we'll "grade" some of the blurbs we studied on Monday and our own drafts. The rest of the class will be a workshop. Make sure to confer with one of the teachers today or tomorrow.

Wednesday's Homework: Finish and type (and save) your blurb. Check it against the blurbs we've studied.

Thursday will be our polishing workshop. We'll start with a grammar minilesson on fragments, sentences, and run-ons. Then we'll look for these (and make corrections) in our own blurbs. We'll also have a workshop. If you haven't already conferred with one of the teachers, meet with one of us today.

Thursday's Homework: *Your author blurb is DUE tomorrow!* Make sure the blurb, along with your picture, looks professional.

FIGURE 3.3. *Author Blurb Genre Study*

EXAMPLES OF STUDENT-WRITTEN AUTHOR BLURBS

Lisa Grey is an author of many popular books for young girls. Copies of her books are sold in both hard cover and paperback. Many of her books such as *A Girl's Journey* and *A Gift from a Flower* have been named bestsellers. She has also received three Newbery Honors. Lisa writes creative stories inspired from her own life. While she was growing up in Ann Arbor, Michigan, she attended high school and worked as a waitress. She has also traveled to Europe, South America, and Australia to view different perspectives of life. After she earned her degree at the University of Michigan, she remained in Ann Arbor to raise a family of her own.

Peter Belden is a writer, sports agent, and a father of two. His novels include *In the Streets* and the Newbery Medal winning *Hoop Dreams*. He is from Ann Arbor, Michigan and attended college at Florida A & M, where he got his degree in business. He is currently living in Mississippi with his wife and loving children.

Nick Jackson, born and raised in Michigan, has always had a passion for drawing cartoons. From the young age of five, he drew stick figures. He later developed his talent into drawing solid characters. In high school, he improved upon his talents by drawing characters in action poses and background features to make his drawings more lifelike. He eventually created his own comic, which became successful later in time. He is now a famous cartoonist with over a hundred published comic books. Nick said, "I'm the best comic book artist to ever come out." He has been crowned as one of the five greatest artists of his time.

Before his recent successes, Nick struggled in life. After completing Michigan Art School, his first job was as a dishwasher for a local restaurant making minimum wage. However, he still worked on his drawing and his comic book. He would make his own comic book by stapling the pages together and selling them on the street. He was discovered by John McIntosh, of McIntosh publishing, who happened to buy one of Nick's homemade comic books. The rest is history. In a few short years, he was at the top of his game with multiple comics already published. His comics were groundbreaking in design, color, and style.

His family has always been supportive of his love for his art. Nick and his family now live in Beverly Hills, California.

FIGURE 3.4. *Examples of Student-Written Author Blurbs*

Standardized Test Writing

Like many teachers, we are concerned about the potential for the kinds of writing promoted by standardized tests to overwhelm writing curricula in classrooms, particularly curricula based in sound pedagogical principles. The story is not a new one, but it continues to amaze us: because of untoward pressures on teachers and schools to measure up, curricula become directly tied to passing state and national tests. And as writing tests strive to assess at least some real writing (as opposed to multiple-choice questions on conventions and style), test makers puzzle out a way to create a prompt that they believe all kids can respond to in a short period of time (usually twenty-five to thirty minutes). All of us who are reasonably well versed in research-based best practices in writing know how far removed this is from everything we know about writers' needs (for time, for response, for choice). And we further know just how difficult this task is that we are asking apprentice writers to undertake: When was the last time you were given thirty minutes to compose a clear, concise, and edited piece on a topic you had never thought about before in a high-stakes environment? Could you pass?

Like many teachers, we struggle between our desire to ignore these demands and our need to find a smart way to help students succeed. We want students to know just how problematic tests like these are, but we also know that for both their benefit and the benefit of schools, we need to find a way to put these exams in their rightful place: so that they do not overwhelm our curriculum, but that they can be seen as just one more kind of writing.

Standardized test writing, then, fits perfectly as a genre study in a classroom, presented as just one more kind of writing that has its own demands, constraints, and structure but that has, at the same time, some variety depending on its rhetorical situation. When we present test writing in this way, we hope we are sending a message to our students that the way they write for standardized tests is not the way they might write for other occasions and purposes, but that they can—with a little preparation—meet the demands of this genre.

We are delighted to see the number of other teachers and researchers who are also turning to this way of approaching test writing. The Michigan Writing Projects have designed a series of units on test writing for elementary students; Katherine Bomer lends her own unique slant on test writing and genre study in her book *Writing a Life* (2005), where she suggests blending students' experiences with memoir study as a way into responding to the writing tests; Gere, Christenbury, and Sassi's book *Writing on Demand* (2005) looks at how to help students prepare for standardized tests. Our own approaches have grown and developed as we have read these important works.

The most vital point about teaching this genre is that we approach it as we would any other genre study. First, we *immerse* students in the genre of test writing, looking with them at prompts, rubrics, and sample responses to the questions. Second, we *inquire* with them about this kind of writing: What are the qualities that cut across those prompts and rubrics? What distinguishes a 2 essay response from a 6 essay response? Who is the audience for this writing? Next, we craft minilessons for *instruction* that help them learn strategies for writing efficiently and clearly in this mode, particularly lessons in organization, theses, and transitional devices. And finally, we help them *integrate* this writing into the rest of the writing they have done in the course: What ideas about good writing transfer? What can they take from their other writing and use in this case?

Through this approach, we have come to believe (albeit reluctantly) a genre study in test writing has some value for our student writers and, when approached in a genre-based way, can help their writing even beyond the goal of passing the test.

1. *Test writing lets us talk about audience in some immediate and compelling ways.* We all struggle to make the concept of audience a real one for our students, from creating situations for them to write to a congressman, a newspaper, or a manufacturer to implementing large-scale research projects intended for specific audiences (such as oral history projects for the community). However, when we talk to students about the *real* audience for the test writing, those folks reading and assessing the tests (and not the manufactured audiences that some tests name), students take notice. "What should you do when you write to an audience who will spend one to two minutes reading your essay?" we ask. "What strategies do you need to implement to make sure they get your point?" Outraged at first by the lack of time readers will spend with their prose (appropriately, we think), students begin to think in serious ways about issues of audience, issues that can then transfer to other discussions about audience that emerge when we study other genres.

2. *Test writing lets us talk about other rhetorical considerations in some immediate and compelling ways.* All those issues of rhetorical situation are easily discussed within this unit and serve as a defining moment when we go on to talk about these concerns for other kinds of writing. For example, it's easy to raise the rhetorical consideration of situation as we talk about the context of test taking and the way you have to adapt your writing process to the real confines (often thirty minutes) of that moment. Purpose? While we dig deeply into the prompts to discover the

stated purpose (e.g., to convince an adult audience of the value of school uniforms), we also take the opportunity to question with them any underlying purposes for the test: to see if they can write in this situation, to see if their organization is good, to see how they can develop an argument. Creation of self as author? These discussions are fascinating ones as students probe the question of truth in their writing. Can they make things up? Can they create a different persona? What is acceptable in this genre, and are those representations of self and situation acceptable in other genres? Again, all of these questions are easily accessed through this genre and help set the stage for full discussions across the other genres we study.

3. *Students gain a lot of confidence as they learn about these tests.* Frankly, one of the horrors of high-stakes writing tests is the excessive amount of stress they have created for students of all ages. Students who have little preparation in this kind of writing are terrified that they won't know what to do. Students who have spent a whole semester preparing for these tests feel unbelievable pressure because they've been overwhelmed with the knowledge of how much these tests count. We believe that approaching test writing as a genre study strikes balance in a world in which these tests are a reality. Students in the composition class told us they felt very prepared for the test and confident in their ability to do well. After this unit, they knew how to read the prompt and analyze it for its most important elements; they knew strategies for writing for the situation and audience; they knew what a 2 essay looks like (and how to avoid it) and what a 6 essay looks like (and how to strive toward it). And, most of all, they were very aware that test writing is just one genre—and not one that would probably be a part of their everyday life outside of these tests.

A Test Writing Genre Study

"Today is a quick write," Sarah announces to the class. "Get out your notebooks. What I want you to do is this: Think about standardized writing tests. Write everything you can remember about taking them: how it felt, what you did. OK? Start."

Silence takes over this normally boisterous class as students write for the full seven minutes. When Sarah asks them to share their memories, student voices fill the room with their despairing feelings about these tests: students say they were frustrated, tired, stressed, uncaring, bored. Angel explains, "Proving something with a lot of details is hard."

Marie adds, "They only give us thirty minutes to structure our thoughts, pick a side, write it up. That's too much to do."

Thus begins our genre study into standardized test writing. Building from the students' experiences, we'll start a two-week study of immersion, inquiry, instruction, and integration, beginning with the prompts.

Studying Prompts

Too often students jump into the writing without looking carefully enough at the prompts attached to these tests. Because this particular class is filled with students from many grade levels, we divide the large group into smaller study groups, each group focusing on the test that is most immediately important in their lives: for sophomores it is the writing portion of the MEAP (the state assessment); for juniors[2] and seniors it is either the SAT or the ACT writing test. This study of various tests will serve our purposes well since students can both study their own test type intently and then look together as a whole class across the three tests to see what is similar and what is different within this genre of standardized test writing.

We begin by handing out the prompts for the three tests (taken directly from their websites) and asking students about the importance of prompts. Marie cuts right to the chase by explaining that the prompt is vital "because if you don't do what they tell you, you flunk." We focus in on the ACT as an example and Sarah asks the students to read the prompt, underline or circle important words, and take notes on important points in the prompt. She explains, "This is an important strategy. When you're in the test situation, you have to take time to do this." She then leads them through a discussion that analyzes the prompt in terms of topic, intended audience, and purpose. They identify the topic immediately but then struggle a bit with the audience and purpose. We delight in their confusion because this is the sticking point of these tests: For whom are you writing these pieces? And for what reason? As students flounder their way through these hard questions, they eventually conclude that the audience must be the people who grade the test. Who are those people? they ask us. Could they, the students, be test graders? As we talk about the qualifications, at least for the state test (in our state, graders don't have to be teachers), they are appalled. "You mean they aren't English teachers like you guys?" And when we

---

[2]At the time we introduced this genre study, we had a specific state test required for juniors. Now those students take a version of the ACT and complete its writing portion.

further explain how much time the test assessors are able to spend on each test (usually one to two minutes), their outrage grows.

We try to turn that anger into a lesson about this kind of writing. Cathy asks, "OK, if you know they're not necessarily English teachers and that they spend a minute or two on your papers, what do you need to do as a writer?" And they get it immediately, yelling out ideas: "Make it interesting"; "highlight points"; "get to the point"; "print so they can read it."

We move on to the next related complexity—the purpose of this kind of writing. One student responds with one level of the answer: "To take a position." Another, though, points out what she sees as the underlying but unstated purpose: "To help them see you're a good writer." Already, they are starting to identify the complicated rhetorical nature of these tests.

For homework (and continued into the next day's class), the students look across several prompts, searching to identify the way the prompts are organized (usually beginning with a situation and then explaining an assignment), the way the directions tend to stay the same while the topic varies (focusing on length of time they'll have to write, urging them to take a position, sometimes specifying the intended audience), the meanings of various verbs (like *support, describe, explore, develop*, and *illustrate*), and the importance of the parts of the prompt that are capitalized or in italics. As we talk about these organizational concerns and continue to refer to topic, audience, and purpose, students focus in on the way the prompts seem to expect the writer to take a particular side of an argument, as if one side is more valued. We talk about what would happen if you disagreed with the implied stance of the prompt and, in fact, wanted to make a different argument. "What might you have to do if you take the unpopular side?" Cathy asks. The students get it right away: "Provide even more evidence."

We end this two-day immersion into prompts with a fun homework assignment for the next day's class: to compose their own prompts for an imaginary standardized writing test. Sarah explains, "Write a prompt for a standardized test. Make your own. How long should it be? Look at the models; it could be different lengths. What will you include?" As the kids respond with ideas about directions, scenario, choice of stance, Sarah goes on, "Good. And there will be a prize. Nick, it's a food prize! Also, a grade is involved."

Students demonstrate their knowledge of the prompts the next day with their smart (and sometimes hysterical) examples of prompts. Each group (the SAT group, the ACT group, and the MEAP group) meets; reads, discusses, and selects its favorite; and presents it to the class. Each group shares its winning entry with the whole class, and the students debate the merits of each, trying to decide which one is most like a real prompt and why.

Angel writes the following, a prompt that has the sound of the typical scientific–public policy samples we've read:

> In some United States high schools, teachers, students and parents believe and have encouraged the school to allow science teachers to teach both Intelligent Design and Evolution. Several parents and students support Intelligent Design because of their religious beliefs, although others believe in Evolution from scientific theories. Evolution believers argue that if Intelligent Design is taught in public schools, there is no longer a separation between church and state. Others support Intelligent Design because they think only teaching Evolution will restrict students' alternative thoughts about how the world was created. In your opinion, should public high schools teach both Intelligent Design and Evolution?
>
> In your essay, take a position on this question. You may write about either both or one of the two points of view given, or you may present a different point of view on this question. Use specific reasons, personal thoughts and examples to support your position.

Lillian creates a prompt that is reminiscent of the ACTs, one that takes on an issue that is both local and of immediate interest to students:

> In some high schools, the districts are encouraged to make it a requirement for students to take two semesters of a personal fitness class. Most parents and teachers support this requirement because they think it will be better for their health. Other parents and teachers do not support it because they think that they should be more focused on their academic classes. In your opinion, should these high schools make it a requirement to take personal fitness throughout their high school career?
>
> In your essay, take a position on this question. Choose one of the two points of view. Use examples and reasons for your position.

Marcus delights the class with his thinly veiled comment on "unprepared" test assessors:

> In this essay you will have the power in your words to discuss your feelings in detail about the test graders. Test graders are people who grade the ACT and SAT. To be a test grader, you need a bachelor's degree and it doesn't matter what your career is. If you have a bachelor's degree you can grade anybody's essays.
>
> So, take a position. If you do have a problem with the way they choose the test graders, express in detail. If you don't, express in detail why you don't have a problem with the test graders.

Use legible handwriting, organize your essay, take a point and back it up, make it interesting with great detail, and last but not least, Good Luck!

You will have exactly 1 hour.

In a free-ranging class discussion following the presentation of each of these prompts, the students talk about how some of them seem more professional than others, some offer too much information, some don't offer enough. They applaud those that give clear directions, clear scenarios, and interesting topics. (And they particularly applaud Marcus' as it captures some of their outrage at the testing situation.) As they discuss these ideas, we see a reinforcement of their growing understanding of the qualities and characteristics of these kinds of prompts.

Working with Rubrics

Because standardized writing tests generally assign a holistic score, one that is explained in a fairly lengthy narrative fashion within a rubric, students sometimes have difficulty identifying the specific categories to which those narratives refer. In other words, both because the rubrics are holistic rather than analytic and because they aren't written in the kind of language that makes sense to many kids (language that transfers to their actual understanding of writing, language that uses terms like *organization* and *voice*), our students sometimes end up a little confused. In order to clear up this confusion, we start this part of the unit with an immersion into the rubrics associated with each high-stakes test in order to answer the question What are these test makers actually looking for?

Sarah begins by putting a test rubric on the overhead and asking students to look at how a score of 1 is described. "What categories seem to emerge?" she asks. Students throw out a variety of answers, but eventually come up with these general categories: topic, content, structure, and grammar. Sarah then explains, "In holistic scoring, it's not really broken down into these categories for a score; you just get a 1," but she emphasizes the importance of understanding these underlying categories as a way to know what the test makers are looking for. Students then go on to look at the rubric descriptions of a 2 paper, a 3 paper, and so on, seeing that the same categories seem to emerge. As students uncover these categories, trying to figure out even more specifics about the qualities the rubrics seem to be seeking, they try to put the test makers' language into their own. The composition class identified a number of qualities that seem consistent and thus important:

- staying on topic

- understanding the question

- taking a side

- providing examples and evidence

- having lots of examples and evidence

- saying it once (not repeating yourself)

- sticking to one idea per paragraph

- using transitions

- having introductions and conclusions

- showing your vocabulary

- using complete sentences

- proofreading

Students take these ideas and go one step further for homework: to describe in their own words what they see as a 6 essay, a 5 essay, and so forth. As the unit progresses and students begin studying sample essays and writing their own essays, we keep coming back to the qualities they have identified, repeating their language so that it becomes second nature to them.

Looking at Sample Essays

As the unit continues, we look specifically at sample essays, interspersing minilessons on strategies and structures for writing essays (such as how to write strong leads, how to use transitions, how to structure this kind of essay, how to integrate details, how to plan the essay), careful reading and analysis of model essays provided on the official websites, and various attempts at writing some of their own. One day, for example, we pass out sample essays without the scores attached. We ask students to read through these essays, consider the rubric and prompts, and score them—and to do so in the two minutes we've explained that real graders have. Students then meet in their study groups to make the case for the score they assigned. Discussion immediately focuses on what you need to do to get your point across to this quick-reading audience. We then talk more in depth about the sample essays, filling in a chart (see Figure 3.5) that helps us identify the specific qualities they notice in essays of different scores. In order to fill in this chart, they have to specify what a 1 lead looks like, what 3 transitions look like, and so on.

Another day we ask students to try what they think is a nutty assignment: to write a 2 essay and explain why, based on the rubric, it should be considered a 2. (This, by the way, is harder than it sounds. When Sabrina suggests that writ-

SAMPLE ESSAYS: WHAT CONTRIBUTES TO A SCORE?
What do you notice about each of the following in the six essays you scored?

	Lead	Examples	Transitions	Introduction	Conclusion
1 Score					
2 Score					
3 Score					
4 Score					
5 Score					
6 Score					

May be copied for classroom use. © 2009 by Cathy Fleischer and Sarah Andrew-Vaughan from Writing Outside Your Comfort Zone *(Heinemann: Portsmouth, NH).*

FIGURE 3.5. *Sample Essays: What Contributes to a Score?*

ing a 2 essay is easy because it just needs to be "raggedy and misspelled," we remind her that she shouldn't make it a 1.) We then ask them to rewrite that 2 essay and turn it into a 6 (an assignment designed to give them both practice in revision and a particular way to work with the specifics of the rubric).

Later in the week, we ask them to try writing the best essay they can on a new prompt they haven't seen before; in subsequent classes, their peers assess the essays as if they were the scorers, spending one to two minutes per paper and explaining in small groups why they gave each score. The unit ends with an in-class practice test in which they have thirty-five minutes to write and ten minutes to reflect on their writing.

What we like most about this unit is the way the students immediately complicate the idea of writing for a high-stakes test. With little prompting on our part, they recognize how the elements of rhetoric affect this genre and figure out what they need to do to "psyche out" the scorers and do well on the test. As a lesson in genre, it serves our purpose well: demonstrating to kids the variations that can occur within even a relatively straightforward genre like high-stakes testing and how much what you write in any given genre depends on your audience, purpose, and situation. (See Figure 3.6 for a general plan for the unit.)

Comics

Scott McCloud, author of *Understanding Comics* (1993), stands at the front of a conference room encouraging a group of K–college teachers to try their hand at making comics. "Start by picking one of these categories: fruit, seasons, presidents, or desserts," he begins. "Then fold your paper into quarters and draw four examples of the category." He cautions, "Don't tell anybody what the category or the examples are. We're going to guess." Although most of the teachers shoot apprehensive looks at each other, his anyone-can-do-this attitude is infectious, and we dig in. We draw lopsided apples and pears and caricatures of Nixon and Lincoln, laughing as we go, but when we sheepishly share our drawings with others, we're surprised (and relieved) at what we find: the drawing doesn't actually need to be very sophisticated to be recognizable; even with not-so-great drawing, it's pretty easy to get your point across through a comic. As Scott takes us through increasingly sophisticated ways of looking at comics and encourages us to think about the connections between story elements and comic frames, the details of drawing and writer's craft, and zooming in and pulling back from the action, we begin to whisper across the table:

"What if we did something like this with the kids this term? Don't you think they'd like it? It would be a great way to get them to think about the

---

GENERAL PLAN FOR STANDARDIZED WRITING TEST UNIT

Part 1:   Introduction to Test Writing Genre Study and Immersion into Prompts
- freewriting on standardized writing tests and sharing
- analyzing ACT, SAT, and MEAP prompts: topic, intended audience, purpose
- developing beginning list of characteristics
- homework: writing a prompt for a standardized test

Part 2:   Understanding Rubrics
- sharing prompts in small groups; comparing with list of characteristics developed yesterday; sharing in large groups and voting for the best
- discussing how those characteristics transfer to rubric
- analyzing SAT, ACT, MEAP rubrics: three ways they're alike and three ways they're different
- rewriting the rubrics in language that makes sense

Part 3:   Connecting Rubrics to Sample Essays
- individually reading sample essays without numbers attached and assigning scores based on the rubric
- meeting in small groups to compare scoring and talk about essays

Part 4:   Writing Practice
- write a "2" essay; revise to make it a "6" essay; discuss experience and observations as a class
- practice writing essay(s) using official practice prompts while simulating official, timed environment
- self-score and/or teacher scores practice essays using official rubric

---

FIGURE 3.6. *General Plan for Standardized Writing Test Unit*

connections between writing and drawing," Sarah asks. "And it might really appeal to some of the artists in the class who don't like writing so much."

"Yeah, but do you really know anything about comics?" Cathy responds. "I certainly don't. Plus, look at this: I can't draw!"

"That's the point, isn't it? I mean, shouldn't we be trying out a genre that is not so familiar to us? Wouldn't that help them understand part of why we're doing genre studies?"

We agree: this is something we will try. The two of us—artistically challenged, non-comic-reading teachers—realize we will truly have to immerse ourselves in the genre, inquiring into it right along with the students, in order to make this work. We recognize it promises to be a true test for us of this notion of the Unfamiliar Genre Project, challenging us to come into class without all the answers, relying on our community of students and teachers to inquire together.

After our workshop with Scott McCloud, we read his book and talked about the ideas he so convincingly explored. And so, even without knowing a lot, we came to see why comic books might be a good genre to explore with the students, an understanding that became even clearer as the unit progressed:

1. *Comics have the potential to appeal to students who are visual learners.* Even as well aware as we all are these days about the idea of multiple intelligences and how that concept affects the many kinds of learners in our classes, we admit that we don't always do as much as we can to create varying learning opportunities in the writing classroom. We knew we had students in the class who were excellent artists and who seemed more visually minded, so we wondered if focusing on a very visual genre would help pull them into writing even more. Could these students see a connection between the writing we'd done so far and the genre of comic books?

2. *Comics provide another means of thinking across genres of communication.* Writing and art have a lot in common. Both are modes of communication, ways of expressing ideas to others. We were interested in exploring with students how these modes were similar and how they varied, hoping that students would start to think about the notion of communication in some productive ways. In other words, we hoped students would recognize that various modes of communication were valid and that understanding more about one might ultimately help them participate in another, the concept we describe as integration.

3. *Comic writer-artists use many of the same processes as other writers.* As we learned more about comic writers, we realized how much their ways of approaching their genre were similar to those of other writers: prewriting, drafting, revising, and editing both their words and their art. We hoped that we would be able to introduce our students to some of the specific processes that comic writers use both to validate the concept of process ("See, even these cool graphic artists use process!") and to inspire them to adapt some of those approaches in their own writing. Storyboarding, for example, is a typical organizing principal for comic book artists; what might happen if our students tried a storyboard as they produced their own comic? If it worked well for them, might it transfer later to their attempts at writing other genres? Could it be a productive strategy?

4. *Comic writer-artists are thoughtful about craft in similar ways to other writers.* Again, as we learned more about the genre of comics, we began to see fascinating parallels between the craft underlying its production and that of other written genres—parallels that we hoped would help the students when they returned to other genres of writing. For example, when comic artists zoom in on a particular moment, moving from a larger picture to focus in on the details of a face or a room, they are using a strategy similar to one we often teach in writing: Barry Lane's (1993) notion of exploding the moment. Just as the strategy of zooming in allows the artist to explore more details of the scene or the person, exploding a moment allows a writer to achieve the same result with words. Would those parallels help our students? we wondered. In particular, would those more visually oriented apprentice writers who struggled with revision find a way in after studying parallel craft in drawing?

5. *Comics draw upon many of the same literary devices students study in literature classes.* Students often struggle with the concepts of literary devices such as symbols, archetypes, and motifs. Although some can spit back the definitions to their teachers (based on years of quizzes about those terms and others), many are confused when it comes to identifying those devices within literature—and even more confused when it comes to using them in their own writing. Visual forms of communication, such as comics, are rife with these devices, we learned. Characters drawn as Prince Charming or a femme fatale or a superhero are easy to recognize and carry much symbolic meaning for our students. Again, we wondered if students might be able to understand literary devices like these more fully through the art of the comics.

An Experiment: The Comics Genre Study

"OK, everyone, this is Scott McCloud, the writer we've been telling you about. Scott's here today to introduce us to our new genre: comic writing." With various degrees of engagement, the students wrap up their conversations with their friends and turn to the guest speaker sitting in the circle by the board.

"I can't draw," one student loudly announces.

"Me neither," pipes in a second. The two of us look around the room, seeing the "show me" looks on the faces of a number of students and wondering if this experiment in the genre of comic books is doomed to failure before it even starts. Scott immediately jumps in.

"Sure you can," he says. "Let's try some things and see." He passes out paper and asks the students to try the same exercise we did with him a few weeks earlier: pick one of the four topics of presidents, seasons, fruits, or desserts and try to draw four examples of the chosen topic. A few students start, complaining loudly about how badly they draw. A few more jump in. Soon, everyone is trying it, laughing at the strange-looking pears and hard-to-discern snowdrifts as they go.

As students finish, Scott takes a few drawings and holds them up, asking the class to figure out which of the four categories each represents. This task easily accomplished, he asks them why some drawings seem a little clearer than others. "How do you know this is a strawberry?"

A student responds, "Because it has those little freckle things."

"Ah," Scott says, "so the little details can help make something recognizable, even if the drawing is not exact." And with these words, they learn their first lessons about this genre: that their drawings don't have to be perfect, that their lines can approximate the object they're trying to depict, and that little details can help make a drawing clearer to an audience. Immediately, the scary genre of comics has been at least somewhat demystified.

Day two brings Scott back again to try another lesson with students. He starts by asking students to focus on their own eyebrows. "Make an angry face," he says. "Feel your eyebrows. Where are they? What are your muscles doing?" Students grimace and touch their faces, shouting out the shapes their eyebrows have taken. "OK, now touch your mouths. What shape does your mouth take in an angry face?" Scott continues to suggest faces to the kids—surprised, fearful, sad, happy, and gross disgust—and keeps asking the students to study what their mouths, eyebrows, eyes, and cheeks do for each expression. They laugh as they look at each other's faces, beginning to notice the way the muscles shape an emotion. "Let's draw some of these. Try to help us identify the expression only drawing eyes, eyebrows, and mouths." Students sketch faces, using what he calls "markers" of each expression. These markers, he tells us, help us know what emotion is expressed, even if the drawing of the face is not perfect.

"OK," he says to the class. "These faces we're working on show what we call the six universal expressions: anger, surprise, fear, sadness, joy, gross disgust. Each face looks really different. I'm going to draw these six on the board, and you copy them down. See what you can do." As Scott sketches the looks, students do as well, amazed at how their placement of eyebrows, lines in the face, mouth, and eyes can truly send a message.

"Most of the expressions we have in the world are some combination of these six. So, let's try some. Can you think of any others?"

"How about worry?" responds one student. Others immediately make a worried face and try to figure out which of the universal traits it combines.

"Maybe mild fear, but also a little anger? Or sadness?" Scott suggests. They go on, exploring various combinations of expressions for evil, suspicion, coyness, and shock, moving their faces and figuring out what the muscles do to portray those emotions.

Scott continues, "OK, let's focus on these five: worry, amused, disappointed, cruel, and suspicious. Practice making the faces and think about how they rely on the universal traits. Then pick one to draw and show to the class."

Students busily get down to work, molding their own faces into different shapes, touching their faces with their hands, and translating that to paper. When it comes time to share their sketches, they're please to realize that the expressions they were trying to create are recognizable to their peers. Day two of immersion in drawing achieves its purpose: students walk away knowing they can do this, knowing that they don't have to be the best artists in the world to make a point through their drawing.

Immersion and Instruction into the Literature of Comics

Over the next few weeks we continue what Scott began: immersing and instructing students in the genre of comics, both in the *drawing* of comics, as described earlier, and in the *reading* of comics. In order to do this, we keep inviting them to jump right in; following the ideas presented in *Understanding Comics*, we try a number of experiments: drawing an object from multiple perspectives (close in and far away, noting the way details are heightened), playing around with frames (those boxes and shapes in which a scene is depicted), and trying out different ways to indicate dialogue, thoughts, and narration (words encased in circles and boxes, often with lines or dots connecting them to characters)—all intended to help even the self-identified nonartists feel more comfortable with drawing. At the same time, we introduce several lessons designed to help students recollect and reflect on comics they have read: from the graphic novel *Maus* (Spiegelman 1986), which most read in ninth-grade English, to comic books they read as kids or as teens. In addition, we bring in comics to look at together. The more we talk, the more students start to understand the complexities and variations inherent in this genre: yes, they can start to identify many of the qualities of comics they learned from their immersion in drawing (the use of graphics and words, devices like frames and thought bubbles, additions like color and detail), but they also start to think about concepts like audience and purpose in the wide variety of comics we study. While this is a stretch for some kids ("I don't ever read comics"), many of those who are regular comic readers have a chance to shine, to offer some fairly sophisticated analysis of this genre they love.

Integration Craft Lessons: Connecting Writing, Drawing, and Literature

As the unit continues, we instruct students through a number of craft lessons, some that focus on the connections between comic writing and other kinds of writing and some that focus on the connections between comics and literature, a movement that not only lets students integrate their insights about comics into the areas of writing and literature but also calls upon their knowledge of writing and literature in order to deepen their understanding of comics. One of the most successful lessons relies on Barry Lane's exploding the moment activity, in which writers slow down the action to draw out details.

Sarah adapts this idea, using an example from Lane's book (a passage written by Jan Wilson), to teach a lesson on using detail in comic writing. In this passage Wilson describes in slow, vivid detail the moment when she poured a full carton of milk over the head of her unsuspecting sister, detailing both the passage of the milk down her sister's face and her sister's instantaneous and livid reaction. Sarah begins by reading the passage out loud. Students break into laughter as they listen to the scene.

"Let's talk about this passage. How long did it take her to do it?"

Allison responds, "One hot minute!"

Kelvin, calling upon some memories from some other lessons he's had in class this term, jumps right in: "She uses snapshots and thoughtshots. They're all there." As Sarah urges him to continue, Kelvin mentions the description of the blond hair. As students point out other examples of snapshots and thoughtshots, they delight in some of the details: *Dadeeee* rather than *Daddy*, for example, and the mention of cocktail glasses and how that suggests a particular time of day.

After a few minutes, Sarah asks, "OK, what's the point of all this?"

Allison immediately jumps in, "You can write about one second."

Sabrina adds, "You can expand it."

"Exactly," Sarah applauds. "So think about this: How would you do this as a comic? Try drawing this scene as a comic. Choose the number of frames you want, the layout, everything we've talked about." Students settle in to try this (with varying success), realizing that in order to truly slow down the action, they'll have to use multiple frames. As they finish up and share, Sarah points to good examples that have used some of the devices they've been talking about in class: the kinds of frames, the level of detail, the way thoughts are depicted, the zooming in and other perspectives. "Next," she tells them, "try this with your own ideas for your comics. Can you use these lessons to stretch out the action and focus on a single moment?" As students begin to sketch and write, they recognize the connections among various genres. Just as they add more frames to the comics they're drawing in order to slow down and stretch out the action, they can use more words, details, and images to do the same in their writing. Yet again, this lesson that we both use in our writing classes all the time takes on a new meaning with students once they envision it through the lens of comics.

The success of another craft lesson emerges almost as a surprise as students make some explicit connections between comics and literature. What starts as an incidental discussion of motifs, symbol, and archetypes and how they might be used in the comics the students are drawing actually helps a number of students make the transfer to those concepts in literature. It begins one day when Sarah is talking through some of the characteristics that will help make the students' own comics excellent. After talking about the necessary components for this unit (ten frames; complete story with a beginning, middle, and end; use of at least some of the techniques they have discussed in class: perspective, facial expressions, words), Sarah raises the question of how best to link pictures with ideas. "How else can you help make the picture show ideas? You might try little items in the background as symbols or motifs."

Kelvin looks confused. "What's a motif? A motive?"

Sarah smiles. "Nope, m-o-t-i-f, *motif*. Who knows what that is?"

Marie makes a stab. "Something that keeps on appearing in the story."

Felise adds, "There's something behind it, like it's symbolic."

Another normally quiet student jumps right in, "It's like in the movie *The Sixth Sense*, the color red keeps coming up."

Clearly pleased, Sarah keeps going, "Good. I'll give you a really easy definition for symbols. Ready? A symbol is something you can touch that represents an idea—something you can't touch."

Marie laughs. "I've heard you say that so much, and I can never remember." As students throw in their ideas about symbols—especially roses as a representation of love—Sarah adds a new idea. "Now, here's another big word. If everyone across the world knows that a red rose means one thing, we call that an *archetype*."

Allison, clearly engaged (for one of the first times this semester), jumps in, "Wait, how do you spell that?"

As Sarah spells the word out loud, a relieved Allison sighs. "Oh, that's not so hard."

Sarah pushes them a little more. "OK, what about this: If I say 'old lady,' what comes to mind, what does she look like?" Students enthusiastically reply, yelling out a lot of ideas: white hair in a bun, glasses on chain, stooped over, comfy shoes. "OK, here's another big word. There's an archetypal character that's called the *femme fatale*. Anybody know what that is?" Again, students jump in: blond, blue eyed, voluptuous, curvy. Sarah keeps the momentum going. "Can you give me another archetypal character? How about a male one?"

Quiet Bradford suggests the superhero.

"Good. Now tell me what he looks like." Students call out cape, short hair, spandex, shorts over tights. Students then name some of the comic book superheroes they know: Superman, Batman, Spider-Man.

As students continue with these thoughts, Sarah turns the conversation back to their story lines, asking them to consider how symbols, motifs, or archetypes might figure into their own comics, how they might integrate these concepts in their drawing. As they return to sketching, it's clear to us that these students have gained a new lens into these literary concepts, a lens that we can see will help them not only in this assignment but when they return to other genres of literature.

When we reflect back on this genre study, we recognize how vital it can be for teachers to venture into unexplored territory. This unit required us to take the plunge as we committed to exploring a new genre that we were neither very familiar nor comfortable with. And, we admit, this was hard work! Future renditions of this unit got stronger and more focused as we adapted the lessons that seemed to work well, reconsidered those that didn't, and developed some new ones. (See Figure 3.7 for a daily schedule of a more developed comics unit.)

But as we look back, we do notice a couple of key points. First, the insights the students offered us were startling at times—particularly, the way they were able to articulate the integration of their learning across to other writing and reading. When we truly didn't hold all the answers, many of the students rose to the occasion, helping us create a true teaching and learning community. Equally important, we were able to experience firsthand the stomach flutters and feelings of inadequacy that can be associated with writing (and teaching) in an unfamiliar genre, feelings that have helped us teach the Unfamiliar Genre Project even better, with more empathy for our students' struggles and more confidence that all our students really can take this on.

SCHEDULE FOR COMICS GENRE STUDY

October

November

Monday	Tuesday	Wednesday	Thursday	Friday
30 Receive pen pal letters! Midterm exam	31 **Minilesson:** Classroom library: comics **My Workshop Plan:**	1 Pen pal letters due **Minilesson:** Define comics **My Workshop Plan:**	2 **Minilesson:** Symbols and icons **My Workshop Plan:**	3 **Minilesson:** Organizing panels **My Workshop Plan:**
6 Receive pen pal letters! **Minilesson:** Facial expressions **My Workshop Plan:**	7 **Minilesson:** Dialogue v. thoughts **My Workshop Plan:**	8 Pen pal letters due **Minilesson:** Showing time **My Workshop Plan:**	9 **Minilesson:** To show or to tell? **My Workshop Plan:**	10 **Minilesson:** Storytelling, plot, conflict **My Workshop Plan:**
13 Receive pen pal letters! **Minilesson:** Psychological landscape **My Workshop Plan:**	14 **Minilesson:** Closure: moment-to-moment, action-to-action, subject-to-subject **My Workshop Plan:**	15 Pen pal letters due **Minilesson:** Closure: scene-to-scene, aspect-to-aspect, non sequitur **My Workshop Plan:**	16 **Minilesson:** Your title, your signature **My Workshop Plan:**	17 **Minilesson:** Revision: reconsider lessons of week 1 **My Workshop Plan:**
20 Receive pen pal letters! **Minilesson:** Revision: reconsider lessons of week 2 **My Workshop Plan:**	21 **Minilesson:** Revision: reconsider lessons of week 3 **My Workshop Plan:**	22	23 Thanksgiving	24
		No school. Your 20-frame comics are due Monday, November 27.		

Minilesson ideas came directly from Scott McCloud's Understanding Comics (1993).

May be copied for classroom use. © 2009 by Cathy Fleischer and Sarah Andrew-Vaughan from Writing Outside Your Comfort Zone (Heinemann: Portsmouth, NH).

FIGURE 3.7. *Schedule for Comics Genre Study*

Unpacking the Unfamiliar Genre Project[1]

WE ARE VERY AWARE, given the multiple ways courses and curricula are structured in individual schools, that not all teachers are able to create a whole curriculum that is genre based, the kind of structure we describe in Chapter 3. Does this mean that you shouldn't try the Unfamiliar Genre Project? That it will be beyond the grasp of your students? Of course not! While we believe a whole-scale semester of genre study is the way to go, we also see the Unfamiliar Genre Project as a viable—and extremely useful—option, even if it represents your (and your students') first attempt at consciously considering genre.

In fact, the very first time Sarah attempted the UGP with high school students, she hadn't yet developed the kind of full semester of genre instruction that she came to in subsequent years (although we think you'd be hard-pressed to find an English teacher who doesn't talk at least some about genre). During that trial year, she introduced the UGP just after her students finished a semester of

[1]An abbreviated version of this chapter was previously published as "Researching Writing: The Unfamiliar Genre Research Project" in *English Journal* (95.4: 36–42). Copyright 2006 by the National Council of Teachers of English. Reprinted with permission.

reading-writing workshop in which they independently pursued their inter-ests—their familiar genres, if you will. And so, as she introduced the UGP to her students, she included minilessons in many of the concepts we've explored in the last three chapters, especially in terms of immersion, inquiry, instruction, and integration. Even without the full base of genre studies she later added to her practice, she found the UGP an important addition to her classroom—so much so that she has taught it every year since 2004, in a variety of ways and in a variety of classes.

In this chapter, we introduce the UGP in the high school setting, drawing from Sarah's multiple experiences teaching it in multiple classes over the last few years, offering suggestions for what you might need if you're taking on the project for the very first time. We share the most current handouts she gives to her students, the assessments she uses, and many of the minilessons she teaches. Then, in Chapter 5, we offer one project as an example of the kind of work her students have produced, a model you can use to discuss the project with your own students.[2]

A Case for the Unfamiliar Genre Project

As we mentioned in Chapter 1, the UGP serves several purposes for high school students: to learn basic research strategies, to engage in a genre study while practicing strategies real writers use to approach new material, to identify the multiple processes writers use to learn about that which is unfamiliar, and to demonstrate that research is a useful tool in creating something students might otherwise think is too difficult.

Perhaps the most important quality of the Unfamiliar Genre Project, though, is that it asks students to use their research by experimenting with and actually writing in the genre they have studied. Applying their newfound knowledge is a critical step beyond research projects that ask students only to present the information they have gathered. Actually using the research, Bloom's taxonomy tells us, cements the ideas and strategies students encounter in this project into their memories (Bloom, Mesia, and Krathwohl 1964). It also provides students with the confidence of having figured out the constraints and demands of particular genres, especially when they next encounter challenging and perhaps high-stakes genres, such as SAT essays or college applications.

---

[2]Throughout the student samples included in these chapters, you'll notice occasions of nonstan-dard English usage and punctuation, as well as certain typographical errors common to student writing. We've retained these in order to illustrate authentic student voices.

An added attraction of the Unfamiliar Genre Project is that its topic is reading and writing. The research topics English teachers offer students too often have nothing to do with reading or writing; this project shines a spotlight on English as a research subject.

Starting Out: First Lessons

"Take out two different-colored highlighters and clear your desk of everything else, please," Sarah announces to a room of talkative ninth graders. "We're going to explore some of your fears about writing today."

Two students shoot worried looks across the room while another pair simultaneously grin, knowing their teacher is up to something. As copies of the introduction to the Unfamiliar Genre Project circulate through the room, Sarah asks students to fold the handouts in half, demonstrating with her copy. The bottom half of the front page consists of a three-column list of writing genres, a version of the list they'll see again later in the year when she introduces the Multigenre Research Project. (See the student handout in Figure 4.1.)

"So far this year, most of you have chosen to write in genres that are either pretty comfortable for you or in genres that we worked on together as a class. Today we're going to start something a little different. For this new project, I want you to purposely choose another kind of genre to write in—a genre that for some reason you find unfamiliar. Here's how we'll start: Using your highlighters, make a key in the margin. Use your darker color for genres you like or tend to write in and the lighter color for genres that are challenging or kind of scare you." As she speaks, Sarah is making her own key on an overhead transparency of the handout.

"Please use your 'like' (darker) color to highlight all the genres you like or tend to write in. Go ahead and work through the list now." Students again shoot looks at each other, seeing what their friends are marking. Soon, however, they are busy at work, marking those genres they have been writing in for most of their lives. "When you finish, pick up your other highlighter and mark the genres you tend to shy away from as well as those you've simply never tried. Not all of the items on your page will be highlighted, and that's OK."

Students keep looking at the list, occasionally asking for clarification. "What's microfiction?"

Sarah opens the question up to the class. "Does anybody know? What does it sound like? Maybe that's one that is worth investigating."

"Now, read through the items you just highlighted—the ones that intimidate or are unfamiliar to you—and circle two or three that are intriguing enough that you're willing to learn more about them. I want you to select genres you aren't familiar with, but I also want you to have fun with this project, so

THE UNFAMILIAR GENRE PROJECT

In your experience as a reader and writer, you've likely encountered more genres than you even realize, but it's also likely that you are drawn to some while you shy away from others. Because we each have distinctive experiences with the many genres we encounter, it's also true that we have our own comfort levels with each genre. (Perhaps you prefer to write fictional stories, or perhaps making up whole stories from scratch seems impossible to you.) In this project, I will ask you to identify the genres that are personally challenging—genres you are not particularly familiar with, that may intimidate you, or that you tend to avoid. From these, I would like you to honestly select one genre that you do not ordinarily choose to write in but would like to learn more about. This project asks you to investigate, read in, and write in a genre that is personally challenging. It has several purposes: to learn to study genres (which you can apply to future genres you will encounter, like college and SAT essays) and to learn *your* research process while *using* your research to create something you might otherwise think is too difficult.

Picking a Challenging Genre

We'll begin this project with honest soul-searching as you pick a genre that is unfamiliar or feels daunting to you. To ensure that you pick a genre that is truly challenging, the quality of the final piece will account for only a small part of your grade on the project; your engagement in the research process and the reflective journal will constitute most of your grade. *See the Unfamiliar Genre Project rubric attached.* A proposal in which you identify your challenging genre along with an explanation of why you chose it and what you'd like to learn is due at the start of class on Friday of this week.

Here are some genres you might consider exploring. Don't limit yourself to these!

advertisement	essay	last will and testament
art commentary	• personal	letter
brochure/pamphlet	• prose	• business
children's book	• literary criticism	• complaint
closing or opening argument	eulogy	• condolence
comic/graphic story	how-to book	• cover
constitution (organizational)	instruction booklet	• to the editor
critique of art/photography	journal article (professional journal)	• of recommendation
economic analyst report	lab report	• to representative

(continues)

FIGURE 4.1. *Project Overview: Unfamiliar Genre Project*

THE UNFAMILIAR GENRE PROJECT *(Continued)*

market report

memoir

microfiction/vignette

newspaper/magazine

- news article
- editorial
- feature article
- in-depth report
- interview
- personality profile
- obituary
- opinion column
- photo-essay
- political/editorial cartoon
- science report
- sports
  - article
  - column
  - season wrap-up

- review
  - book
  - CD
  - concert
  - movie
  - play

novel or novella

parody

photo-essay (w/captions)

poetry (many kinds—pick one)

- ballad
- cinquain
- epic
- free verse
- haiku
- ode
- sestina
- slam/spoken word
- sonnet

- two-voice
- others!

psychological evaluation

public service announcement

resume

satire

scrapbook

script

- commercial (TV or radio)
- monologue
- radio play
- screenplay
- skit
- soliloquy

short story

speech

song (lyrics with music)

technical report

user's manual

The Research Journal

Although research includes many steps, the order of these steps may vary, like in writing. You may want to jump right into a draft. You may prefer to begin by reading (and collecting) samples of your genre. Perhaps you will begin by journaling: you might first deal with your fears by putting them to paper. To some extent, this project is intended to allow you to discover your own research process, which you'll write about in your reflective letter. Whatever your process, metacognition (thinking about your thinking) is an important part of this research project. Throughout this study, keep a journal (handwritten or typed—your preference) of your experiences. *Use this journal to keep track of*

FIGURE 4.1. *(Continued)*

your daily activities as well as your feelings about each stage of the work. You'll write about your metacognition in your reflective letter. Please write in this journal each time you work on the project.

Reading in Your Unfamiliar Genre

One part of your research in this genre study is to simply read within the genre. You must collect the best five to ten samples of published work in your chosen genre that you can find. (This means that you will be reading more than five to ten samples!) Once you've chosen your models, carefully reread them as you think about (and take notes on) the writer's craft, structure, and unique strategies in each piece. You'll create an annotated bibliography listing each of these models along with an annotation for each. Finally, consider what the collection as a whole teaches you about the genre: What are its characteristics? Where are its boundaries? In what ways does this genre borrow from other genres? In what ways do other genres borrow from this? You'll synthesize these big-picture observations in the reading portion of your reflective letter.

How-to Book

In class, we'll analyze some aspects of writing: audience, purpose, content, organization, presentation, voice, word choice, sentence fluency, proofreading, and other writing minilessons. We'll keep our notes from this analysis in a how-to book that we'll discuss together, but you will individually track your chosen genre. This how-to book, which will count toward your homework grade during the unit, will serve as a planning tool for writing in your genre and a resource as you write your annotated bibliography.

Annotated Bibliography

An annotated bibliography is a formatted list of your model samples (bibliography) with a paragraph of thoughtful observations about the way each model sample was written or crafted (annotation). You will write an annotation for each of the model samples you collected for your genre. Notice in the rubric for this project that your annotated bibliography is worth 20 percent of the project grade. It is important that you pay as much attention to writing your annotated bibliography as to writing your centerpiece (also worth 20 percent of the project grade).

Writing in Your Unfamiliar Genre

The centerpiece of this project, of course, will be a finished piece in your chosen (challenging) genre. You must take this piece through several drafts including parent, peer, and teacher conferences (required). Before you actually get

(continues)

FIGURE 4.1. *(Continued)*

THE UNFAMILIAR GENRE PROJECT *(Continued)*

---

to your final piece, it's likely that you'll experiment with the genre—you may have several starts before you write the piece you will finish for your final project. *Keep all of the writing (drafts, false starts, conference notes) you accumulate throughout this project.* As you are writing, be aware of what you are doing: How did you write in this genre? What were your influences? What writer's tools did you use? You'll synthesize these observations in the writing portion of your reflective letter.

Reflective Letter

The last piece you'll write for this project is your reflective letter. Consider your experience over the weeks of this project. Reread your journals. Reread your drafts and experimental writing. Reread your notes on your reading. With all this in mind, think about what you've learned about reading in this project. What have you learned about writing? What have you learned about studying genres and researching in general? Your reflective letter should discuss your experiences with reading, writing, your research process, and metacognition. In each of these sections, make big-picture conclusions from your experience.

Letter from an Interested Adult

As you know, I think it's really important to share your hard work with your parents and guardians. When you are completely finished with your Unfamiliar Genre Project, share it with a parent, guardian, or another interested adult and *ask him or her to write a letter to you* in response to your work.

Research Binder

The final project will take the form of a research binder. It should be typed, organized, and easy to navigate. Your binder should include the following (make one tab for each category):

- centerpiece and reflective letter (including all four sections: reading reflection, writing reflection, research process, and metacognition)
- research (metacognition) journal (with dated entries)
- experimental writing, all drafts, and all conference notes
- copies (with reading notes) of the best five to ten samples of published work in your chosen genre
- parent/guardian letter

May be copied for classroom use. © 2009 by Cathy Fleischer and Sarah Andrew-Vaughan from Writing Outside Your Comfort Zone *(Heinemann: Portsmouth, NH).*

Figure 4.1. *(Continued)*

you should select your genre with these criteria: unfamiliar but interesting." Discussion slowly breaks out as students contemplate, privately and aloud, whether they will choose a genre that is truly unfamiliar or pick something "safe." To capture this dilemma, Sarah asks students to write about the options they are considering and work through the pros and cons of each. She uses this opportunity to introduce the research journal, a key component of the UGP, for which they have just written the first entry. This first journal entry has a second purpose: it serves as their entrance ticket to the library the next day, where they will conduct a presearch to ensure that they can find plenty of examples that they *want to read* in their chosen genres.

Thus, the project begins: a project that asks students to identify a genre they find challenging; to gather, read, and analyze model examples of that genre; to identify key characteristics of that genre; to write in the genre; and to keep a research journal in which they think through the project and attempt various drafts. And because the idea is for students to honestly select a genre that is foreign or intimidating, we repeatedly assure them throughout the process (and in the rubric) that this is primarily a research project, and although original writing in their chosen genre will be the centerpiece of the presentation, the writing's quality will be worth only a fraction of the final grade.

By the end of the multiple weeks devoted to the project, students will present their projects in a research binder containing sections for the following:

1. their best draft of original writing in the studied genre

2. a reflective letter on how the final piece demonstrates their research as well as what they learned in the roles of reader, writer, and researcher

3. a how-to book that captures the essence of their genre as well as their application of the minilessons throughout the project

4. all experimental writing, drafts, and conference notes

5. an annotated bibliography of five to ten samples that they read in their chosen genre with an analysis of the craft (conventions, style, structure, traits, strategies, and so forth) within the piece as well as its quality

6. their research (metacognition) journal

7. a letter from an important adult with whom they chose to share their project

In the pages that follow, we explain step-by-step how the students get from this first-day minilesson to that culminating binder. Beginning with some ideas for how to make the UGP fit into your own context and schedule, we go on to share the thinking behind, the minilessons for, and some student samples of the major components, in the general order Sarah introduces them to students: the research journal, the project proposal, the collection of sample genres, the how-to book, the annotated bibliography, the centerpiece writing in the genre, the reflective letter, and a letter from an important adult. At the close of this chapter, we also explain our rationale for and approach to assessing these projects.

Creating a Schedule That Fits Your Context

Over the next four to nine weeks (depending on the nature of the class, the purpose for the project, the time available), the high school students will spend at least half of their class time and much of their homework time working on the UGP. Class periods are devoted to library visits, lessons, and workshops. The teacher-led lessons involve introducing expectations, presenting selections of sample projects that the class analyzes for strengths and weaknesses, demonstrating how to keep a research journal, practicing how to identify genre conventions by reading examples, role-playing conferencing strategies, writing annotations, and formatting a bibliography using MLA style. In addition, at least one day a week is devoted exclusively to workshopping this project.

We've included two sample schedules here (see Figure 4.2), just to give you some idea of what planning for the UGP might look like: one for a no-frills four-week version and one for a more extensive nine-week version. The four-week schedule is the most compressed we can imagine. This version allows you and the students to work through all the component parts, but we want to stress that it truly is the no-frills version. It not only leaves no extra time for other parts of your English curriculum, but also leaves out what we think is essential to the research process: time to think, browse, play, explore, even procrastinate (in that thinking-about-the-project-but-not-yet-sure-what-I'm-doing sort of way). This compressed schedule also doesn't allow for the flexibility we all need to deal with the realities of unplanned weather days, assemblies, counselor visits, and reteaching, as well as individual students' planned and unexpected absences.

More typically, and especially if the class has not been organized as a series of genre studies, Sarah spreads this unit out over an entire nine-week marking period, pairing it with a novel study or some other unit that runs alongside the UGP, which gives students time to reflect on the UGP and take a break into some other aspects of the curriculum. For example, in a junior-level English course, Sarah teaches the UGP in the third quarter. For a few weeks, Sarah devotes the beginning of each week to preparing for high-stakes tests in a mini genre study, as described in Chapter 3, while teaching the UGP during the last three days of each week. When the test prep is finished, she replaces it with another mini genre unit. Alternatively, once in a Short Readings course, Sarah's entire class studied

THE UNFAMILIAR GENRE PROJECT: FULLY COMPRESSED (THE FOUR-WEEK VERSION)

Monday	Tuesday	Wednesday	Thursday	Friday
Introduction 1 **Introduction to UGP:** Highlighter activity **Minilesson 1:** Metacognition and your research journal **Minilesson 2:** Set up research binder, tabs	Introduction 2 **Minilesson:** Browsing **At the Library:** Presearch online and in the stacks **To Do Today:** • Find samples online. • Find samples in stacks. • Print/check out copies. • Write proposal.	Introduction 3 **To Do Today:** • research strategy scavenger hunt	Introduction 4 **Idea Workshop Proposal DUE** at the end of the period. **To Do Today:** • Search for and read samples. • Finish writing proposal.	Annotated Bibliography 1 **Minilesson 1:** What makes it a *model* sample? **Minilesson 2:** Mini genre study: MLA bibliography entries **DUE** by end of the period: one model sample bibliography entry in MLA style.
Analyzing Craft 1 **Lesson:** News article inquiry (game)	Analyzing Craft 2 **Checkpoint:** Bibliography of five model samples **Lesson:** How-to booklet	Analyzing Craft 3 **Lesson:** How-to booklet	Analyzing Craft 4 **Checkpoint:** Annotated bibliography **Lesson:** How-to booklet	Workshop 1 **Minilesson:** What is experimental writing? **My Workshop Plan (computers available):**
Annotated Bibliography 3 **Lesson:** Mini genre study: Immersion and inquiry into annotations	Annotated Bibliography 3 **Minilesson:** Writing annotations **To Do Today:** • Write your annotations.	Review Sample Projects 1 **Lesson:** Analyze strengths and weaknesses of sample projects	Review Sample Projects 2 **Checkpoint:** Experimental draft **Minilesson and To Do:** Analyze strengths and weaknesses of your (and classmates') projects	Workshop 2 **Minilesson:** Conferring **My Workshop Plan (computers available):**
Workshop 3 **Minilesson:** Organize your binder, tabs **My Workshop Plan (computers available):**	Workshop 4 **Minilesson:** Writing your reflective letter **My Workshop Plan (computers available):**	Workshop 5 **Minilesson:** Proofread your project! **My Workshop Plan (computers available):**	Workshop 6 **Minilesson:** Asking an important adult for a reflective letter **My Workshop Plan (computers available):**	**Unfamiliar Genre Project DUE** Museum walk. Read and write a reflective letter to *three* classmates.

May be copied for classroom use. © 2009 by Cathy Fleischer and Sarah Andrew-Vaughan from Writing Outside Your Comfort Zone (Heinemann: Portsmouth, NH).

Figure 4.2. *The Unfamiliar Genre Project: Two Versions*

THE UNFAMILIAR GENRE PROJECT: FULLY EXPANDED (THE NINE-WEEK VERSION)

Monday	Tuesday	Wednesday	Thursday	Friday
Introduction 1 **Introduction to UGP:** Highlighter activity **Minilesson 1:** Metacognition and your research journal **Minilesson 2:** Set up research binder, tabs	Introduction 2 **Minilesson:** Browsing **At the Library:** Presearch online and in the stacks **To Do Today:** • Find samples online. • Find samples in stacks. • Print/check out copies. • Write proposal.	Introduction 3 **To Do Today:** • research strategy scavenger hunt	Introduction 4 **Idea Workshop** **Proposal DUE** at the end of the period. **To Do Today:** • Search for and read samples. • Finish writing proposal.	Introduction 5 **Minilesson 1:** What makes it a *model* sample? **Minilesson 2:** Mini genre study: MLA bibliography entries **DUE** by end of the period: one model sample bibliography entry in MLA style.
		Analyzing Craft 1 **Lesson:** News article inquiry (game)	Analyzing Craft 2 **Lesson:** Make how-to booklet, content v. craft (pp. 1–4) **My Workshop Plan (computers available):**	Workshop 1 **Checkpoint:** Bibliography of five to ten model samples in MLA **Minilesson:** What is experimental writing? **My Workshop Plan (computers available):**
		Analyzing Craft 3 **Lesson:** How-to booklet: audience and purpose (pp. 5–8) (Remainder of time devoted to another topic)	Analyzing Craft 4 **Lesson:** How-to booklet: organization and presentation (pp. 9–12) **My Workshop Plan (computers available):**	Workshop 2 **Checkpoint:** Experimental draft **Minilesson:** Conferring **My Workshop Plan (computers available):**
		Analyzing Craft 5 **Lesson:** How-to booklet: voice and word choice (pp. 13–16) (Remainder of time devoted to another topic)	Analyzing Craft 6 **Lesson:** How-to booklet: presentation and style (pp. 17–20) (Remainder of time devoted to another topic)	Workshop 3 **Checkpoint:** Notes from at least two conferences **Minilesson:** Taking and ignoring revision advice **My Workshop Plan (computers available):**

Workshop 4 **Checkpoint:** Lead and alternative lead **Minilesson:** Finding and fixing run-on sentences **My Workshop Plan (computers available):**	Analyzing Craft 7 **Lesson:** How-to booklet: leads (pp 21–22) (Remainder of time devoted to another topic)	
Workshop 5 **Checkpoint (at end of period):** Annotated bibliography **My Workshop Plan (computers available):**	Annotated Bibliography 2 **Minilesson:** Confer first-draft annotations **To Do Today:** • Write your annotations.	Annotated Bibliography 1 **Lesson:** Mini genre study: immersion and inquiry into annotations **To Do Today:** • Write your annotations.
Workshop 6 **Minilesson:** Organize your binder, tabs **My Workshop Plan (computers available):**	Review Sample Projects 1 **Lesson:** Show and tell—analyze strengths and weaknesses of a sample project (or focus on samples of one section)	
Workshop 7 **Minilesson:** Writing your reflective letter **My Workshop Plan (computers available):**	Review Sample Projects 2 **Lesson:** Show and tell—analyze strengths and weaknesses of a sample project (or focus on samples of one section)	
Unfamiliar Genre Project DUE Museum walk. Read and write a reflective letter to *three* classmates.	Workshop 9 **Minilesson:** Asking an important adult for a reflective letter **My Workshop Plan (computers available):**	Workshop 8 **Minilesson:** Polishing your final draft **My Workshop Plan (computers available):**

Figure 4.2. (*Continued*)

memoir as their unfamiliar genre and expanded the unit to study memoir collectively and independently throughout the week (see more about this version of the UGP in Chapter 6). The point here, of course, is that no one knows the particular demands of your course, your students, your school, and your curriculum like you do. The two model calendars in Figure 4.2 are only frameworks to help you start imagining a plan for your version of the Unfamiliar Genre Project. You might want to try one of these or something in between.

The Components of the UGP

Making the Invisible Visible: The Research Journal

As we mentioned previously, students start one of the most important parts of the UGP—the research journal—on the very first day of the project, as they jot notes about the genres they are considering pursuing over the next few weeks. Students keep up with the research journal throughout the project, noting their developing ideas and reflecting on their learning. As explained in the introductory handout to the UGP,

> Although research includes many steps, the order of these steps may vary, like in writing. You may want to jump right into a draft. You may prefer to begin by reading (and collecting) samples of your genre. Perhaps you will begin by journaling: you might first deal with your fears by putting them to paper. To some extent, this project is intended to allow you to discover your own research process, which you'll write about in your reflective letter. Whatever your process, metacognition (thinking about your thinking) is an important part of this research project. Throughout this study, keep a journal (handwritten or typed—your preference) of your experiences. Use this journal to keep track of your daily activities as well as your feelings about each stage of the work. You'll write about your metacognition in your reflective letter. Please write in this journal each time you work on the project.

Sarah tells her class, "Think of the research journal as a place where you can record what you did today, but more importantly, pay attention to what you noticed, what you learned." Sometimes, in the early stages of the project, she offers students prompts to get their daily journals started. Here's one guided research journal prompt that has been particularly useful:

- 5 minutes: What is the best piece you've ever written? (Or think of one you're proud of.)

- 5 minutes: How did you write it? What was your process?

- 5 minutes: What techniques did you use to craft that piece?

- 5 minutes: How could you apply these successes to the piece you are writing for the UGP?

Why do we push this reflective component so strongly? All students should learn to be conscious of and evaluate the internal dialogue we all engage in as we think, read, write, and learn. The teacher's job is to introduce useful skills and strategies; the students' job is to try out these skills and strategies and find a process that works for them as individuals—in other words, to find which research tools work best for them. This notion of metacognition becomes very concrete in the UGP as students begin to understand that they have the power to learn about that which is unfamiliar and that they can employ this power with or without a graded assignment. A core intention of this project, then, is to nudge students toward lifelong learning.

As students move through the project, they write entries in their research journals that are designed to document their reading, false starts, and approaches while evaluating how each method worked, how it felt, and what they noticed as they were reading and writing. We want students to reflect on frustrations as well as successes so that they might begin to determine what their own processes look like. We also want students to internalize the common wisdom that the process, far more than the result, is key to learning.

Min explains the value she found in the research journal:

> One of my main fears was how I was to tackle such a big piece. From writing my trouble out, I dissected it piece by piece. . . . I tried my best to write every day, but I usually wrote a long one every two, three, four days. . . . [I wrote about] the ups and downs of what seemed to flow, what didn't flow and suggestions to self. Over mid-winter break, I went to NYC/Baltimore; I made connections to my project and quickly penned them down as well. I treated it almost like a writing diary!

The research journal, as you'll see, is a key component to the project: it serves as one section in the final binder and as the basis for students' reflective letters and how-to books (two other components, described later in the chapter). (See Figure 4.3 for an example of a student's research journal.)

Committing to a Genre: The Project Proposal

After that first day of students thinking about unfamiliar genres and coming up with a possible genre for exploration, Sarah introduces the concept of immersion.

SAMPLE RESEARCH JOURNAL OF ANNA MARIA LIST, WHO STUDIED CHILDREN'S BOOKS

February 5, 2008

	Children's Book	Microfiction	Political/Editorial Cartoon
Pros	• Very easy access to published samples • Get to draw pictures! • Doesn't take a long time to read many samples • Even though they're for kids, they're still fun to read	• Short • Can read a lot of samples in a short time	• Get to draw pictures!
Cons	• No picture books in the media center • Could be boring after a while	• Short—must capture all of the story elements in few words • Not very common—may have trouble finding many samples • Every single word matters (not much room for mistakes) • Sometimes I don't get the deeper meaning	• I'm not that interested in politics • Not very "in the know" on current events

February 8, 2008

The first step I took in researching for my Unfamiliar Genre Project was to narrow down my focus. I was undecided about whether to study chapter books for older children or picture books for younger children and their parents. So I went to the public library and started picking books at random. I read the standard ABC books, chapter books, storybooks with pictures, etc., but I also read a book written in a very innovative style that I hadn't seen before. It was *The Music of Dolphins* by Karen Hesse, which was a longer book without pictures, much like a chapter book,

Figure 4.3. *Sample Research Journal*

but it was written entirely in poems. The whole book was a collection of short poems that all complemented each other, but each one could have stood on its own as a single poem. I thought this type of children's book was very interesting and new, but I could not find any other books in this style.

From my selection of books, I decided that I would rather do picture books for younger children than chapter books for older children, firstly, because I enjoyed the illustrations so much, and secondly, for the ability of a picture book to communicate an idea or feeling with such a short and simple plot. *The Giving Tree* by Shel Silverstein, for instance, really evoked a strong feeling in me, despite its very simple plot and simple sentence structure. Or maybe it was *because* of its simplicity.

After I finally decided that I wanted to study picture books, I browsed through the picture book section in the library and checked out as many as I could carry to read at home. Thus, the first phase of my research process came to an end.

February 11, 2008

Things That I Noticed by Reading A LOT:

After coming back from the library, I spent a few days just reading the books that I borrowed. From the samples that I checked out, I noticed many things that I failed to note when I read picture books as a child:

- I like storybooks for older children who know the basics of reading, but still like to be read to. This would rule out ABC books, color books (like *Brown Bear, Brown Bear, What Do You See?*), number books, etc. Nothing really happens plot-wise in these books, so I don't find them very exciting or entertaining.
- Many books that I read had rhyming patterns. They were almost like really long poems. I'm not sure if I like this, but I suppose that the rhythm while reading out loud could be nice to listen to.
- Some books had "deeper meanings," or messages that could be interpreted differently by an older audience, probably parents. I found this very clever, because the book could be read on different levels, and if a child grew up with a book like this, he/she could discover something new every time he/she read it.
- Some books were original ideas from the authors, and other books were retellings of folktales or stories that the author heard from somewhere else. I found that the retellings tended to have more morals, with unpleasant consequences for the characters that were not morally sound.
- Some books had very elaborate illustrations, whereas other books had very simple and minimalist illustrations. I'm not sure which ones I like more yet.

(continues)

FIGURE 4.3. *(Continued)*

SAMPLE RESEARCH JOURNAL OF ANNA MARIA LIST, WHO STUDIED CHILDREN'S BOOKS *(Continued)*

February 15, 2008

After reading for several days, I went back to the public library to expand my small collection of picture books. I found some books by Shutta Crum, a local author. I read her first novel, *Spitting Image*, some years ago and I really liked it, so I checked out all the Shutta Crum picture books in the library and read them at home.

After I read the Shutta Crum books, I noticed that the one that I liked the most was not an original idea from Shutta Crum; it was a retelling of a folktale. It is called *Who Took My Hairy Toe?* and Crum heard it on a recording of Walter McCanless, who heard the tale from his wife, who heard it from a Southern African American in 1882. This means that the folktale probably originated in the Southern storytelling tradition, according to Crum.

The most noticeable difference between *Who Took My Hairy Toe?* and the rest of Crum's books was the general feeling that the book evoked. In the end of *Hairy Toe*, the main character is snatched away, screaming, by a red-eyed hairy monster on account of his tendency for theft, and the readers are warned not to steal. In Crum's other books, such as *The Bravest of the Brave*, and *All on a Sleepy Night*, the ending is a happy one, with the main character tucked safely into bed with loving family members surrounding him. Both of these books were original ideas that Crum thought of herself, and the difference is obvious. I prefer the darker tale of the old man in *Who Took My Hairy Toe?* to Crum's more pleasant stories, for the excitement, and I think if I read *Who Took My Hairy Toe?* a decade and some ago, it definitely would have made me scared (in a good way) and exuberated.

February 21, 2008

After reading several more picture books, I noticed another thing that was common in a lot of children's books. Many children's books are written in rhyming fashion, almost like the entire book is a long poem with a stanza on each page. I wasn't sure if I liked this, but the more I think about it, the more clever it seems to write in this style.

First of all, picture books are meant to be read out loud by parents or guardians or older siblings, etc. to young children who are just learning how to read. The rhyming scheme would create a rhythm that would entice the child to listen, much like a song would. Also, the child might be encouraged to follow along and look at the words, and thus the child would be able to associate a certain spelling pattern with a certain sound. Dr. Seuss

---

FIGURE 4.3.   *(Continued)*

employs this method effectively in many of his books, such as *The Butter Battle Book*, *Sleep Book*, *The Lorax*, and *The Cat in the Hat*.

This is also true of onomatopoeias. *All on a Sleepy Night* by Shutta Crum, for example, uses onomatopoeias for sounds that are heard in the night, as well as rhyming format for a narrative. While read out loud, the book sounds very rhythmic, and it is very easy to follow along.

Although I was not sure if I liked rhyming children's books at the beginning of my research process, I have now decided that the style is very clever, and a great way to help children learn to read, which is the main purpose in writing a children's book.

February 23, 2008

I read a few more children's books in the past few days, and I have noticed a pattern in the books that I enjoy significantly more than the others. Many of these are also award winners or honorable mentions for the Caldecott Medal or the Newbery Medal. These books had simple plots and simple narratives that could easily be understood by a child, yet these books also spoke to older age groups, such as parents, older siblings, guardians, or 17-year-olds doing genre studies. This, I believe, is the key to writing a book that is interesting to both the child and the parent who is reading the book to the child.

One of my favorite books from when I was very young is Shel Silverstein's *The Giving Tree*. I loved this book when I was much younger, and I reread it yesterday from when I checked it out from the library. Much to my surprise, I almost loved the book even more than when I was younger. I was afraid that I would read the book now and realize what a terrible story it is, like when I watch my favorite movies, such as *Free Willy*, from when I was a kid. But when I reread *The Giving Tree*, I saw nuances in the story that I hadn't recognized before. The story of the tree giving up everything that she had just to please the boy spoke beyond the context of the tree and the boy; it showed the strength of unconditional love. This is the kind of message that people of all ages can relate to, and I think this is why *The Giving Tree* is such a good example of a well-crafted children's book.

March 4, 2008

I have decided that as my final project, I will write a retelling of *Androcles and the Lion*. I first read this story in Latin class one or two years ago, and it has really stuck with me. The great thing about this tale is that it ends without anyone dying or getting eternally cursed. These are trends that [I] see a lot in most retellings.

(continues)

FIGURE 4.3.   *(Continued)*

SAMPLE RESEARCH JOURNAL OF ANNA MARIA LIST, WHO STUDIED CHILDREN'S BOOKS (Continued)

Androcles and the Lion has a happy ending, so the moral is not "if you do this, then this horrible thing will happen to you," it's "if you do this, then this wonderful thing will happen to you." This is a really significant difference, and little kids would also relate to this moral because it turns a monster into a friend.

March 5, 2008

I was at the library, so I went online and printed out these three versions of *Androcles and the Lion*. The second one is closest to the one that I translated from Latin, and it is also the one that I think I will base my version off of.

March 9, 2008

I started writing my first draft of *Androcles and the Lion*. I decided that I could change the name "Androcles" to "Andy" to make the story more applicable to modern names. I don't know if this really makes a difference, but "Androcles" just seems too formal and stuffy for me.

One really difficult thing I have encountered is how to put my own personal twist on the story. I need to add something different and new to make the story interesting, even though it is so incredibly old. Writing a children's book is beginning to be a lot harder than I expected.

March 12, 2008

I read my draft to our table in class, and they all seemed to like it. I didn't get as much constructive criticism as I hoped for. Everyone agreed with me that the story needs more dialogue to liven it up, but other than that, nobody suggested any drastic changes. Not that I am raggin' on my group or anything. I guess sometimes a first draft can be dang close to a final draft.

March 20, 2008

My conference with Ms. Andrew was totally different than with my group. She suggested that the nickname "Andy" have an explanation for the deviation from "Androcles," and she also suggested that I put in a new character to give him his nickname. I think this is a really great idea, because it will not only enrich the story, but it will make it totally new and fresh when compared with all the other retellings of *Androcles and the Lion*.

I conferenced with my dad today too, and he said that if I included a new character, it should be Andy's mother. I think this is exactly what I will do. Things are looking up; the story is improving!

FIGURE 4.3.　*(Continued)*

March 24, 2008

I finished editing my second draft, and I think I am really close to my FINAL draft. The words flow pretty well throughout the story, the plot makes sense, I put my own personal little twist in the tale. One thing that I have not given much thought to is the illustrations. I think the illustrations got left on the back burner for awhile, when I was focusing so much on the story and the text.

From my reading and researching, I've found that I really like Ian Falconer's style of illustrating. He works mostly with black and white, but occasionally he puts in a splash of bright vivid color. This really appeals to me, and I also like that his drawings are fairly simple, yet they are still beautiful to look at. I think I will use this style in my story.

March 27, 2008

When we were first assigned the Unfamiliar Genre Project, I thought that I would choose to immerse myself in novels, short stories, satires, or some other genre that I deemed highly "intellectual." However, the more I thought about it, the more I felt myself gravitating towards children's books. Sure, I have read a lot (and that's an understatement) of children's books in my life, but I asked myself, have I ever analyzed a children's book? In all my impressively long history of reading children's books, I always read picture books for pure pleasure. I never delved below the shiny laminate illustration on the pages to examine the thinking, planning, research, and underlying messages that are required for a successful children's book.

I am very satisfied with my final copy of Andy and the Lion. I chose to illustrate the book with simple drawings and occasional vivid splashes of color, which I think will appeal to children's imaginations. I think it is evident that I painstakingly researched and read books in the genre, and I genuinely believe that the story is well-rounded.

FIGURE 4.3.   *(Continued)*

We usually find that our students are unused to the kind of immersion we want them to try in the early stages of this project—taking their time, browsing, and enjoying themselves as they explore a new genre. Thus, Sarah begins the UGP with a day in the library, where students can search in the stacks and online for samples of their chosen genre that they *want* to read—a first step toward committing themselves to a particular genre and gathering the five to ten samples in that genre that are required for the project. Sarah, though, wants students to clearly understand that immersion involves more than going to the library and grabbing the first samples they see. So she begins with a minilesson about browsing: Sarah models how she browses by, as Nancie Atwell recommends, "taking the top off of her head" (1998, 331). She demonstrates her browsing patterns by leading students to the section of the library reserved for short story collections. She talks aloud to them about her impressions of each book she pulls off the shelves as she reads the lead, skims the table of contents, and then flips through the book, noticing the presentation, the author blurb, and other techniques she uses for judging whether or not she is interested in each book, and then decides whether to return it to the shelf or to add it to the pile she will check out from the library. Throughout, she talks about how she chooses and suggests that if students notice that some samples in a genre interest them and others do not, that's probably an indication that they are beginning to discern which samples will be their models; if they can't find samples they want to read, they might want to look again at their highlighted list and consider another genre to study. As students begin their browsing, a number of them do switch their initial genre choice on this day; Sarah encourages them to continue spending sufficient time this first week deliberately and thoroughly browsing, pointing out to them that this is the time to decide on their genre of study. Once this week ends, she explains, they will not be allowed to switch their focus.

In addition to giving students time to browse and think about their unfamiliar genre choices, Sarah devotes time this first week to explaining the expectations for the project, encouraging them to locate their resources and write about their experiences in their research journals. Partway through the week, Sarah introduces a lesson designed to help students take an inventory of where they are in the project, what resources they have gathered, what resources they still need to gather, and where they might find even more resources. Students enter class to find the "Genre Scavenger Hunt" handout on their desks (shown in Figure 4.4).

This scavenger hunt has proved particularly successful for a couple of reasons: as students race the clock to see who can find the most answers, laughing as they go, we're reminded that students always appreciate learning that has been turned into a game, especially a game like this that is both fun and offers some very specific instruction in how to explore their unfamiliar genre (instruction that, of course, can transfer to all kinds of research). In addition, as students work individually on the scavenger hunt, Sarah gets some time for one-on-one conferences, giving her an opportunity to check early on for deeper understanding. Sarah's school has the advantage of a portable laptop lab on wheels, allowing her to provide each student with a computer to work on. Although it's not essential, access to the Internet adds to the enthusiasm students bring to this lesson.

GENRE SCAVENGER HUNT

1. What's your genre? Does it go by any other names?

2. Who are some famous or well-known authors/writers of your genre? (Name as many as you can.)

3. Where might you find information on the Internet about your genre?

4. What key words and phrases might you type into a search engine to find samples of your genre?

5. How and where might you find instructions for how to write in your genre on the Internet?

6. Where in the library might you look for samples of your genre?

7. Where in the library might you find instructional materials for how to write in your genre?

8. If you don't know where to find information in the library, whom or where might you ask for help?

9. Is there any other place (bookstore, television, parent's office, etc.) where you could find samples of your genre? Where?

10. Is there any other place (local newspaper, parent's office, teacher, etc.) where you could find help writing in your genre?

11. Who are some *local* authors/writers of your genre? (Name as many as you can.)

FIGURE 4.4. *Genre Scavenger Hunt*

This immersion into the project expectations and time to browse helps students prepare for their first formal writing of the UGP: the project proposal. Due at the end of the first week, the proposal lets students finalize their decision about which genre they will pursue for the next several weeks and celebrate their learning thus far. In order to write the proposal, students respond to the following questions:

- Which genre would you like to read and write in for your Unfamiliar Genre Project?

- What experiences, if any, do you have with reading or writing in this genre?

- What do you already know about this genre?

- Why are you choosing this genre?

- What would you like to learn by studying this genre and completing this project?

Given the presearch strategies in which they've been engaged for a full week, students generally find writing the proposal an easy task. (See Figure 4.5 for a sample student proposal.)

Inquiring into Sample Genres

"Now that we've decided on our genres and had time to begin some exploratory reading, I want you to be more purposeful with your reading into your chosen genres," Sarah announces as she walks around the room at the beginning of the next week, handing out copies of a fictional news article she's written for today's lesson (shown in Figure 4.6)[3]. "This week we're going to have a series of lessons designed to help you read into your genre. That is, we're going to try to shift our attention from *what* your reading says to thinking about *how* it is said."

For the first lesson in this series, the class begins by talking about defining characteristics: What makes a news story, for example, different from any other genre? As the class brainstorms a few obvious and more subtle characteristics, Sarah marks them on an overhead of the handout: columnar layout, short (often one-sentence) paragraphs, paragraph-long stand-alone quotes.

When it is clear that students are picking up the idea of defining characteristics, she then divides them into small, heterogeneous groups for an inquiry game. "The object of the game is to find the most characteristics of news arti-

---

[3]Students especially enjoy this ficitional piece authored by Notta Real Person because many of the names in the article are real: including their principal Arthur Williams.

SAMPLE PROJECT PROPOSAL BY MOLLY BOND

Which genre would you like to read and write in for your Unfamiliar Genre Project?
I want to focus on personality profiles. I want to write about my good
friend . . . who recently had knee surgery and doesn't know what will happen with
her athletic career.

What experiences, if any, do you have with reading or writing in this genre?
I have no experience with writing personality profiles.

What do you already know about this genre?
I know that you have to focus on one person and you interview the person and
their friends and family.

Why are you choosing this genre?
I want to do another sports-related article, but I also think [my friend] is an
amazing person and friend and would be interesting to write about.

What would you like to learn by studying this genre and completing this project?
I would like to be able to learn how to go about writing a good profile because
knowing how to write different ways makes you that much more of a better writer.

FIGURE 4.5. *Sample Project Proposal by Molly Bond*

cles, no matter how small," Sarah announces to the groups. "Here are the rules:
For every characteristic you mark that no other group has noticed, you earn a
point. You can block other groups from earning points by noting the same observations. Any questions? Are you ready? You have ten minutes. Go!"

As she mills around the room, glancing at students' lists, she encourages
the kids, reminding them that no detail is too minute. Eventually, she gives a
two-minute warning and prepares to record all of their observations as well as
the team scores on the list begun at the start of the period. Before the class is
over, she also makes sure to leave enough time to distribute a second handout
(shown in Figure 4.7), a copy of the original handout with the addition of
thirty-six observations specific to news stories that she has identified. They
compare the class list with the noted observations and applaud their items that
aren't included on the handout. As no group yet has come up with as many

News Story

As you read the following news article, think about its defining characteristics—what makes it a news story as opposed to a fictional story or an essay or a poem or a movie review? **Note your observations in the margins around the article.**

Community service requirement "a better idea than expected"

➡ **Notta Real Person**
Reporter

After getting off to a rough start last spring, the community service requirement at Huron is gaining acceptance by staff and students.

"I never thought the community service project would fly," senior Eric Doe said. "But once I realized that I wasn't going to get out of the requirement, I decided to try to have fun with it."

With the help of Social Studies Teacher Stu White, students have initiated community service projects from tutoring elementary students to painting murals to raking leaves around the community.

"I knew that without strong teacher support, this program was going to have a tough time

Huron junior Eric Doe helps Logan Elementary student Tim Yu with an art project.
Photo by Kim Smith

surviving," White said. "The idea behind the program is too important to let it die."

However, not all students feel the requirement is worthwhile.

"I just don't see how raking some lady's leaves is educating me," sophomore Eric Evans said. "This whole thing is pointless."

Principal Arthur Williams presented the community service requirement to teachers in 2002. After three and a half years of negotiating and planning, the requirement was instituted for all grades last spring.

"After the controversy of getting started, I'd say people now believe this is a better idea than expected," Williams said.

What could you learn about writing news stories from reading this article?

FIGURE 4.6. *Sample News Article*

Anatomy of a News Story

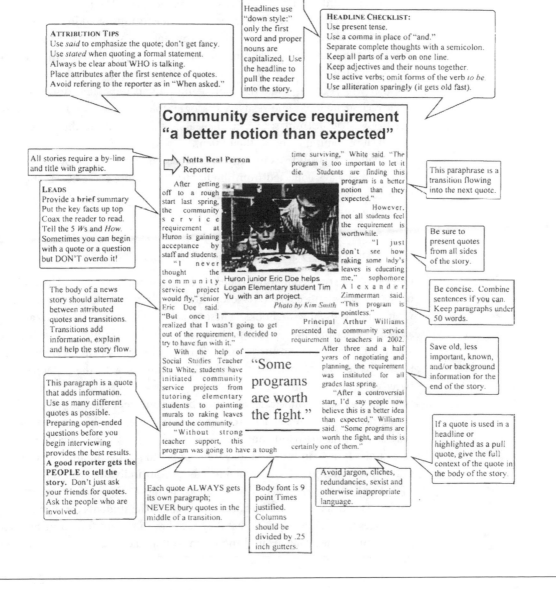

ATTRIBUTION TIPS
Use *said* to emphasize the quote; don't get fancy.
Use *stated* when quoting a formal statement.
Always be clear about WHO is talking.
Place attributes after the first sentence of quotes.
Avoid refering to the reporter as in "When asked."

Headlines use "down style:" only the first word and proper nouns are capitalized. Use the headline to pull the reader into the story.

HEADLINE CHECKLIST:
Use present tense.
Use a comma in place of "and."
Separate complete thoughts with a semicolon.
Keep all parts of a verb on one line.
Keep adjectives and their nouns together.
Use active verbs; omit forms of the verb *to be*.
Use alliteration sparingly (it gets old fast).

All stories require a by-line and title with graphic.

LEADS
Provide a **brief** summary
Put the key facts up top
Coax the reader to read.
Tell the 5 *W*s and *How*.
Sometimes you can begin with a quote or a question but DON'T overdo it!

The body of a news story should alternate between attributed quotes and transitions. Transitions add information, explain and help the story flow.

This paragraph is a quote that adds information. Use as many different quotes as possible. Preparing open-ended questions before you begin interviewing provides the best results. **A good reporter gets the PEOPLE to tell the story.** Don't just ask your friends for quotes. Ask the people who are involved.

This paraphrase is a transition flowing into the next quote.

Be sure to present quotes from all sides of the story.

Be concise. Combine sentences if you can. Keep paragraphs under 50 words.

Save old, less important, known, and/or background information for the end of the story.

If a quote is used in a headline or highlighted as a pull quote, give the full context of the quote in the body of the story.

Each quote ALWAYS gets its own paragraph; NEVER bury quotes in the middle of a transition.

Body font is 9 point Times justified. Columns should be divided by .25 inch gutters.

Avoid jargon, cliches, redundancies, sexist and otherwise inappropriate language.

Community service requirement "a better notion than expected"

→ **Notta Real Person**
Reporter

After getting off to a rough start last spring, the community service requirement at Huron is gaining acceptance by staff and students.

"I never thought the community service project would fly," senior Eric Doe said. "But once I realized that I wasn't going to get out of the requirement, I decided to try to have fun with it."

With the help of Social Studies Teacher Stu White, students have initiated community service projects from tutoring elementary students to painting murals to raking leaves around the community.

"Without strong teacher support, this program was going to have a tough

Huron junior Eric Doe helps Logan Elementary student Tim Yu with an art project.
Photo by Kim Smith

time surviving," White said. "The program is too important to let it die. Students are finding this program is a better notion than they expected."

However, not all students feel the requirement is worthwhile.

"I just don't see how raking some lady's leaves is educating me," sophomore Alexander Zimmerman said. "This program is pointless."

Principal Arthur Williams presented the community service requirement to teachers in 2002.

After three and a half years of negotiating and planning, the requirement was instituted for all grades last spring.

"After a controversial start, I'd say people now believe this is a better idea than expected," Williams said. "Some programs are worth the fight, and this is certainly one of them."

"Some programs are worth the fight."

FIGURE 4.7. *Sample News Article with Observations*

notations as there are on the handout, they are amazed and impressed with what one can find when one looks carefully at a text—and this is a simple, two-hundred-word piece!

As students are quick to point out, Sarah's version should be better; after all, she is experienced and comfortable with newswriting. Their work, they note, will be harder with an unfamiliar genre. We agree! The point of the lesson is that through the course of their research, students must read in their selected genres first *to become familiar* with the conventions, structures, layout, style, voice, strategies, and other defining characteristics used to craft them. Later, after students have analyzed and compared multiple samples of their chosen genres, they will begin to make the more complex and important discovery that while each genre looks and reads in a recognizable way, professional writers do not follow strict formulas; in fact, their ability to complicate the genre while keeping it recognizable marks their talent.

Sarah expects students to perform a variation of this lesson on each of the samples they have collected from the library and to use these observations to write each annotation for the required annotated bibliography, a lesson they'll learn on another day (described later in the chapter).

Beginning with the End: How-to Books

One of the most concrete ways students pull together their new understandings of the qualities and characteristic of their genres for this project is through what Sarah calls how-to books. These small student-made booklets are designed to give students a structured space to put their findings about the nuances of the craft behind their genres. Through a series of minilessons, Sarah lays out a specific format for these books, beginning with the difference between content and craft.

"For today's lesson, clear everything from your desk except one sample of your genre and the news article from yesterday's game," Sarah announces at the start of class. As she hands out six sheets of plain paper and thin markers to each student, she continues, "Today we're going to start pulling together some of the observations you've been making about your individual genres."

"The first step is an art project," she continues. "We're going to put all of our observations into a how-to book." Sarah walks the students through folding their pages hamburger-style, so that they each have a twenty-four-page booklet. Staplers make their way around the room so that each student can place two staples in the spine of his book.

Sarah asks students to title their book *How to Write a _____ by _____*, inserting their chosen genre and their own name (e.g., *How to Write a Short Story by Yasmeen Mohammad*). As she gives students a bit of time to use the markers to make fancy covers, she walks around the room to help make sure staples are in place. This time also helps resistant students begin to soften to the idea of their task: to deconstruct this genre they've only begun to study and that, by nature of the project, is unfamiliar to them.

When she's sure every student has a stapled book, Sarah begins: "Open your how-to book to its first facing pages. Label the left side, the inside cover, 'page 1' with the title 'Content: What Your Reading Said.'" (See Figure 4.8 for the first few pages of one student's how-to book.) On the board, she has drawn a mockup of the facing pages to help students visualize this process. "It's really important for the layout of this book that your notes on these pages face each other. Label the right page 'page 2' with the title 'Craft: How They Said It.'" This distinction between content and craft is an easy concept for some students, but others need a concrete illustration. It's easiest to use a short, common text in a familiar genre for this illustration. (Sarah often uses the news article from the previous day's game; in the student sample we offer here, she used an article from *English Journal* titled "Don't Blame the Boys, We're Giving Them Girly Books," by St. Jarre [2008].) Together, the class brainstorms (as Sarah records the observations on the board) what the common text is about and then begins a discussion of how it is written, moving between the two pages as students begin to discern the difference between content and craft. Students copy these notes onto pages 1 and 2 of their handbooks. When using the news article from the inquiry game as the example, Sarah helps students fold and tape the second handout (with all of her annotations in the margins) directly onto the second (right-hand) page.

The class finishes the period with time for each student to label the next set of facing pages in the booklet "Content in [my sample's title]" and "Craft in [my sample's title]." (In the student how-to book included here, her sample's title is *Rich Part in Life*.) The remaining class time and their homework is devoted to applying today's discussion to the model sample (in their chosen genre) they brought with them to class; they are to distinguish between what their sample says and, very generally, how it is written.

On the following day, students bring more samples of their genre and their how-to book to class. As the class settles in, Sarah winds around the room, checking that they understood the difference between content and craft for their own sample (their homework on pages 3–4). On the board, she has drawn diagrams of two sets of facing pages and numbered them 5 through 8. Also on the board (off to the side, in a section that will not be wiped clean), she has a table of contents for the how-to book that she expects will guide her minilessons for the next few weeks (as shown in pages 1–4 of Figure 4.9).

They begin class with a general discussion of their experiences with their homework and a review of the differences between content and craft.

"Now that we've shared our observations from last night, I'd like for us to think carefully about some of the decisions writers make when working. We're going to walk through some of the considerations writers ponder. First we'll

Content

dfn— what it's about (ideas)
   ideas
   topic
   information, facts

In "Don't Blame the Boys":

opinions on reading lists,
curriculum
sexism, bias, stereotypes
what he considers girly
definitions, characteristics
counterarguments
angle

1

Craft

dfn: how it is written, style, eloquence.
   persuasiveness
   effectiveness

word choice   tone
audience   organization
sentence structure   voice
grammar   length
punctuation   rhetoric (audience+
                              purpose)

In "Don't Blame the Boys"

① citation

no evidence
sexist word choices
SAT essay — audience = interested adults
rant   (offered English teacher)
counter arguments
5 P style, w/ body's P split up
Voice— casual + professional (mixed)
          pretentious
relevant
   (sources!)

2

Content

In the <u>Rich Part In Life</u>:

• the value of money
• the value of death
• the value of life
• Changes after people are exposed to
   wealth
• human psychology after losing a
   loved one
• maturity
• family (biological, no blood ties)
• public / private life
• alcoholism
• possession (of anything)
• fantasy (dreams) vs. reality
• dependency
• truth vs. lies
• denial
• personal discovery (of themselves)
• regret

3

Craft

In the <u>Rich Part In Life</u>:

• enjoys foreshadowing elements
   (introduces characters earlier
   than they are formally introduced,
   but sparks reader's interest)
• language is simple — to fit the narrator,
   a young boy in his early teens
• metacognition — boy's thoughts are being
   thought about, many of the paragraphs
   are written in that fashion
• the voice is young — but the tone & ideas
   written about are much more developed —
   demonstrate's the boys maturity
• written to prove the point that family
   does not change even if wealth does —
   uses characters in the book to illustrate.
   this fact
• At the beginning of a paragraph, no indenta-
   tion
• Describes the body language as a way
   to show the character's emotions
• Uses the character's unseen environment
   as a description of/source of the maturity
   level that he is at
• Not long sentences, no Hawthornean
   type descriptions

4

FIGURE 4.8. *From "How to Write a Novel" by Min Liu*

HOW-TO BOOK CONTENTS

Page	Title
1	Content: What Your Reading Says
2	Craft: How They Said It
3	Content in [genre sample's title]
4	Craft in [genre sample's title]
5	Audience
6	Audience in [genre sample's title]
7	Purpose
8	Purpose in [genre sample's title]
9	Organization
10	Organization in [genre sample's title]
11	Presentation
12	Presentation in [genre sample's title]
13	Voice
14	Voice in [genre sample's title]
15	Word Choice
16	Word Choice in [genre sample's title]
17	Sentence Fluency
18	Sentence Fluency in [genre sample's title]
19	Proofreading and Style
20	Proofreading and Style Considerations in [genre sample's title]
21	Leads
22	Lead in [genre sample's title]

FIGURE 4.9. *How-to Book Contents*

discuss what these are, then we'll think about how each relates to your particular genre, and finally we'll think about how you will deal with each in the piece you are writing."

You'll notice that Sarah has adapted several of these considerations—listed in the table of contents—from Vicki Spandel's *Creating Writers Through 6-Trait Writing Assessment and Instruction* (2001). Just as we hope teachers will create their own versions of the Unfamiliar Genre Project, Sarah has made adaptations to the six traits rubric. As we discussed in Chapter 3, her version renames some of Spandel's categories, emphasizing the variations in each trait depending on the genre at hand. The how-to book demonstrates for students in a hands-on way how those variations play out in their chosen genre.

Several of the two-page spreads in the how-to book then are devoted to a specific trait of writing: content, organization, presentation, voice, word choice, sentence fluency, and proofreading. The goal for students will be to identify what the trait means in general terms, and then identify the specifics of that trait for their genre, much as they just did with the content versus craft distinction. (Notably, proofreading is largely the same among genres, but Sarah calls her students' attention to the special style considerations that relate to individual genres: the differences between Internet and print, journalistic style, or MLA, for example.) Other pages in the book are devoted to other considerations for writers: audience and purpose, leads, and any other writing mini-lessons Sarah plans for the unit. (Any additional writing lessons you want to include will require additional pages in the booklet; it's best to plan ahead for this scenario!)

The general procedure for introducing any of these traits or considerations is the same: "Let's start on page 5 of your how-to book. Go ahead and label that page 'Audience,'" Sarah narrates as she models it on the demonstration-size version she drew on the board. "So—remind me what audience is again," she teases as she segues into the lesson.

"It's the reader," Brendan pipes up.

"OK. Do you pay attention to who your reader is when you're writing?" The students give examples and little stories about considering their audiences. "And what about the readers' expectations? What do they need? What do they want from this piece? What will they be looking for?" Sarah leads the class to think about the newspaper example, and students are quick to identify the school's students as its primary audience, dependent on their attitudes toward the implications of the service-learning proposal. They also cite teachers, administrators, and parents as secondary or tertiary audiences.

"Now look at one or two of your model samples. Who is the audience for each?" Sarah continues, "Remember to label the sample you're using." As students begin reading and writing, they ask questions that lead them to complicate the idea of audience as they consider the notion of multiple audiences for their sample pieces. We sometimes share with them an example of multiple audiences you may remember from Chapter 3—when students discovered that standardized test writing could have primary and secondary audiences. While the test makers identified one audience for the students to address in their writing (an imaginary school board, for example), the students quickly realized that the real audience was the assessors of the test.

"Now, I'd like for you to think about the draft you're about to write. Who is your audience? In which publication do you imagine your piece will appear?" Students draw a line across the bottom of the two-page spread and make notes about their own audiences and the needs of those audiences. (See pages 5 and 6 of Figure 4.10 for sample pages of another student how-to book. On page 5, the class analyzed a classmate's poem entitled "Best Friends by Default.")

As students finish, Sarah continues: "Audience quickly leads us to purpose, which we'll explore on page 7. So, what do we mean when we talk about the purpose of your writing?"

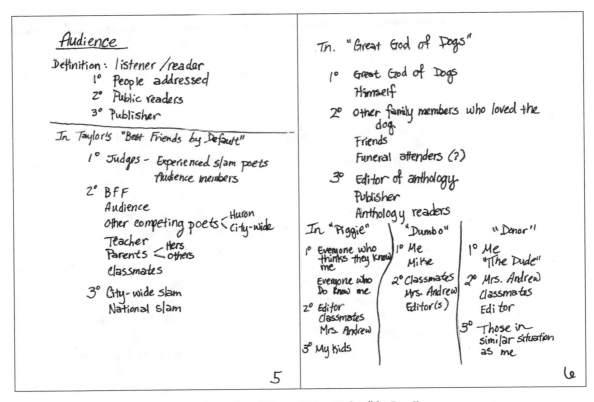

FIGURE 4.10. *How-to Book Pages on Audience from "How to Write a Eulogy" by Ran Ji*

For each of the two-page spreads in the how-to book, Sarah is careful to draw characterizations out of the students rather than explain the definitions, to help them construct their own understandings of the concept. Then, they analyze the class example (such as the newspaper article) before she sets them off on their own to examine the model samples they are using and finally to think about how they are or will address each area in their own draft. Sarah tends to pair related concepts (audience and purpose, organization and presentation, voice and word choice, presentation and style) in fifteen- to twenty-minute minilessons over the next weeks. She reserves the rest of each class period for workshop in which students are allowed to find and follow their own research and writing processes. Five minutes before the class is due to end, she announces the time and encourages students to make an entry in their research journals. "Write about what you did today, but more importantly, write about what you noticed, what you thought about as you were working."

In addition to helping students recognize the distinctive qualities of their own genre, the how-to books help students understand the qualities of good writing that extend across genres. Brendan expresses this understanding when he writes in his research journal: "The How-To booklet reminded me that photojournalism is not so different from other genres, even feature articles and opinion columns. For example, a photo essay hardly has any written words, but it still uses leads like all other articles—the leads are simply pictures and captions instead of quotes and paragraphs."

Putting It All Together: The Annotated Bibliography

Perhaps the most traditional part of the UGP is the preparation of an annotated bibliography. We believe students should know how to use a bibliographic form, but—as any of us who teach research skills knows—it can be difficult to make lessons in bibliography lively and exciting for students. By staying consistent with a genre approach to teaching, however, Sarah has figured out a way to keep students invested and make these entries come alive. Sarah designs her lessons on writing annotations as a mini genre study: the class collectively immerses itself in past students' work, inquires into how the annotations were written, receives some instruction about annotated bibliographies, and discusses ways in which annotations are similar to and different from other genres the students use.

On the first day of this series of lessons, Sarah provides a handout with a variety of student-written annotations from past UGPs (see Figure 4.11). Some of these samples are stronger than others, which reinforces students' awareness that they can learn not only from what's included in a piece of writing but also

---

VARIOUS STUDENT ANNOTATIONS FOR THE UGP

What makes an annotation *good*? As we immerse ourselves in these samples of the genre, inquire into how each was written. Ask yourself: What in this sample is helpful to me? What else do I want to know? How was this sample put together? What can I learn from this sample? How does it compare with the others? (The following annotations were written by high school students for the Unfamiliar Genre Project and are directly quoted from their projects, errors and all.)

Bailey Yi: Political Pamphlets

Paine, Thomas. "Common Sense." *Archiving Early America*. 2008. Archiving Early America. 21 Feb 2008 <http://www.earlyamerica.com/earlyamerica/milestones/commonsense/text.html>.

One of the most influential pamphlets in American history, Paine's Common Sense is most certainly a masterpiece of persuasion and coercion. In his eloquence, Paine leads the reader from the concept of natural rights to the Bible to the contemporary state of American affairs. As you arrive at the end of the piece, you would not carry any doubt of Paine's assertions, for the path from which you came has become narrower and narrower, to a point where all possible objections are addressed and the opinion thoroughly supported. It is as if Paine was building this piece up for such an effect. This piece is an excellent example of a well-written political pamphlet, and helped me immensely with composing my own.

Brian Li: Novels

Sebold, Alice, *Lovely Bones*, New York: Back Bay, 2004.

The book probably influenced me the most even though I did not read all of it. I liked the approach of the future going back. I like the fact that everything has already happened when the story starts and the main character looks back and describes things. Later it turns into the present tense.

(continues)

FIGURE 4.11. *Handout on Various Student Annotations for the UGP*

VARIOUS STUDENT ANNOTATIONS FOR THE UGP *(Continued)*

Notes (in brief)

- First person
- Tragic
- Romantic
- A different blend of different things, lots of items in the story
- Suspension keeps the reader waiting

Allison Reid: Sports Columns

Martin, Jason A. "Yankees Mystique Over?" Self Published 30 Apr. 2007. 12 Feb 2008 <http://www.sportsbettingbaseball.com>.

This is included because, quite frankly, it is absolutely terrible (a "what not to do"). Jason A. Martin does take a strong stand but then awkwardly alternates between informal and formal tone. The story, if it can even be called one, states that the New York Yankee's aura is becoming more ordinary and less elite than it has been in the past. But Martin is unsuccessful at backing up his accusations. Since when do two trips to the World Series in less than seven years mean failure? The article leaves the reader with brows furrowed, working much too hard to decipher Martin's meanings. It's no wonder he's self-published.

Chelsea Froning: Songs

Colton, Graham. "Best Days." *By Graham Colton.* Rec. 24 July 2007.

This song has a more complicated accompaniment part than many of the songs I have been listening to, but it sounds deceivingly simple. The melody is in a major key in the chorus, but in a minor key in the verses. As a result, the song sounds mellow and a little sad. The lyrics are basically reminiscing about past good times, and saying that you should enjoy the present. This is a fairly typical topic for songs, but it is always catchy and appeals to the audience. It is organized as more of a speech than a story, because the singer is trying to convince the

FIGURE 4.11. *(Continued)*

listener to enjoy the present, which causes the song to have a persuasive presentation. The word choice and voice are informal and simple, which makes the song seem more typical and still appeal to the listener. I would like to try to incorporate the switching between major keys and minor keys into my writing.

Chris Berloth: Movie Reviews

Example #2 The Forgotten
Written by: James Berardinelli

The more I read the review the less I enjoyed it and the less I thought it covered the main points that it should have. All this author does is destroy the movie the entire time, he doesn't talk about the cast much, he defiantly doesn't talk about the comparison to other movies, and never says weather he thinks the plot was original or not. I believe that all he had intentions to do was to take all the bad thoughts about this movie he could and put them into writing. I believe the reason he left out certain points is because it would make the movie look better then what he thought it was. Isn't a movie review supposed to tell people about the entire movie, not just the bad parts?

Albert Cheng: Parodies

Animal Farm—

This book is a very famous parody of the Russian Revolution that I believe we are going to read [in class] very soon. This is also one of the few parodies that isn't concentrating on humor, but instead, is concentrating on telling what happened during a historical event. Another thing that separates this parody from others is that it uses animals to represent the historical figures. I found this technique of substituting animals for humans very amazing. Any reader who knows anything about the Russian Revolution will immediately start making comparisons of Napoleon to Stalin, Snowball to Trotsky, Old Major to Karl Marx, etc. because the author, George Orwell, has done such a great job writing this book. However, as great of a literature work Animal Farm is, I really didn't get much out of it that would help me write my own parody because my story is based on humor and a fairy tale, not a great historical event.

Figure 4.11. *(Continued)*

from what is not present. Together, Sarah and her students discuss the content as well as the craft of each sample annotation, compiling a list of what an annotation is, what it typically includes, and how to write one. Just as they have done with other genres, they are quick to discern the differences between those annotations that are useful and those that are less so.

Sarah closes the class by asking students to transfer what they've learned from this first lesson to their own attempt at annotations. "Tonight's homework is to start a first draft of the annotations for your five to ten model samples. You'll have two nights to do this, but it's a lot of work, so I don't want you to put it off. At the beginning of class tomorrow, I'll check that you have at least two annotations written and then you'll have a complete first draft due the following day. Tomorrow we're going to practice conferring our annotations, so I want you to be realistic about what a good first draft looks like."

As promised, the next day Sarah walks around the room, checking students' progress and handing out copies of a first draft that one of her students wrote, which the class is about to discuss.

"OK, you guys, here is a sample of a first draft of an annotated bibliography by Katie that we are going to look at together." (See Figure 4.12.) "Yesterday we looked at some examples of annotations. For our second day of looking at annotations, we're going to look at this strong first draft while thinking about writing our own annotations. Think about this draft in terms of What do I like? What is useful to me? What would I like to know more about? What would I encourage the writer of this annotated bibliography to add?" She has moved to the front of the class, where an overhead of the handout awaits on the projector.

"So here's the title of Katie's draft: 'Annotated Bibliography: Independent Genre Project.' *I* would like to know which genre we're talking about here, and so in the title I would like to know that it's for an in-depth feature," Sarah models as she starts out the whole-class conference. The room is silent as students copy Sarah's notes and visibly search for something to say.

"What is the first thing that you notice, just looking at the page? Not having read a thing on the page yet, presentation-wise, what do you see?" Sarah encourages.

"It's single-spaced," a voice calls out.

"One paragraph per annotation."

"It's not indented. There's no tab."

"That's right. The whole paragraph is indented. How does that look to you?" Sarah encourages.

"It's easier to read."

SELECTIONS FROM KATIE STRODE'S ANNOTATED BIBLIOGRAPHY

Annotated Bibliography

Independent Genre Project

Altman, Lawrence K. "The Feud." New York Times 27 Nov. 2007.

<http://www.nytimes.com/2007/11/27/health/27docs.html?ref=science>.

> This article is about a feud between two doctors that started when one used an artificial heart from the lab of the other in a transplant. I think it sits on the line between news and feature articles, because it tells a story and there's a lot of extraneous information. However, it is also pretty newsworthy because the feud just ended—that's the reason the article was even written.

Kantrowitz, Barbara, and Julie Scelfo. "What Happens When They Grow Up." Time 27 Nov. 2006: 47–53.

> The 'they' that the title of this article refers to is autistic adults. It's not specifically about one person, but it does refer to several different people continually throughout the article. This seems to be a common way to write a feature article that focuses on a group of people. It's fairly long, at seven pages, and includes lots of graphics, photos, and pull quotes. There is also a shorter, related article included near the end, which also seems to be a common thing to do with feature articles. This article was the cover story.

Kluger, Jeffrey. "What Makes Us Moral." Time 3 Dec. 2007: 54–60.

> This article, also a cover story, is six pages long and has lots of graphics. It's written in a way that doesn't refer to the time or date, but it's probably fairly recent, given the up-to-date research that it refers to. The article could have been written two weeks ago or two months ago—it's ambiguous in this way. Like feature articles tend to be, it's a 'soft' news story. It's not about an event, but rather something that people might find interesting.

FIGURE 4.12. *Selections from Katie Strode's Annotated Bibliography*

"It's almost like when you have an outline and you have main information and the smaller point indents in."

"That's an important observation. You all are doing great! Big picture: Anything else about the presentation?" Sarah asks.

"MLA."

"First the citation, then the paragraph."

"Yes. Good. And how about this?" Sarah circles the first letter of each entry.

"The entries are in alphabetical order."

"What if there wasn't an author?" Sarah asks.

"Then you just go by the first letter of the title."

"For a first draft, how does it look?" Sarah wraps up.

"It looks good."

"Really good."

"I agree," Sarah says. "OK, so let's look at each of the works cited. You can tell the writer used an MLA helper site. It's all consistent and has all the needed information."

"It's not just lists of the websites."

"Yes. Remember that yesterday we had some examples that just gave the title of the sample, and maybe the author's name, and we decided that's not enough. If I were having a conference on a draft like that, I would recommend that they get it into MLA style," Sarah says.

"OK, so now let's look at an actual annotation." She begins reading aloud: "This article is about a feud. . . ." As the class discusses three of the annotations in this first draft, Sarah is careful to draw advice out of the students rather than lecture at them.

Based on this discussion, Sarah's students come up with this list of recommendations for writing annotations:

An annotation should:

- be a four- to ten-sentence paragraph

- summarize the article's content in the first sentence or two and then comment on that content; the rest of the annotation should comment on how the sample was written

- discuss how the sample influenced you, or what it taught you

- discuss how the sample was written, its craft—that's the whole point

- discuss the point of view of the sample

- not cover every single aspect of how the article was written, just the important or influential ways; if you don't have something to say, don't pretend—just explain why you put this sample in your bibliography

- focus on what was either really good and/or really bad about the sample

- be really specific; it's OK to give examples from your sample as long as you give your reader enough information to understand you

- act as a kind of a minireview; your opinion belongs in an annotation

The next day, Sarah's students confer on a first draft of their annotated bibliography with a small group of classmates. As the minilesson on this workshop day, Sarah shares with the class the revision of the previous day's first draft (shown in Figure 4.13). They are impressed with how much this strong draft improved, based on the class' comments.

Drafting the Centerpiece: Putting Research in Action

These experiments in how-to books and annotated bibliographies are intended to help students break down the genre, but also to serve as—albeit complex—prewriting activities. In producing both documents, students have to think hard about the essence of their genre and articulate the qualities that help define that genre, a first step toward composing their own piece. In other words, their immersion in the nitty-gritty of their genre and their instruction in how to read the craft of their genre helps students feel comfortable with what was previously unfamiliar. The next step, then, is to demonstrate their new understanding by composing their own attempt at the genre in question. Sarah runs this part of the project as a typical writing workshop: students work largely on their own and at their own pace as they move through various stages of their writing process to pull together their best attempt at writing in the genre. Over the years students have impressed on Sarah just how fundamentally important it is that they write their centerpiece in this unfamiliar genre on a *familiar* topic, one they are committed to, one they care deeply about. Chelsea, who wrote an original song, speaks to many students' experiences:

> I had no idea where to start with writing my own melody or my own words. . . . [But] after figuring out what my song was going to be, I had no trouble writing first the chorus, then the verses of my final piece. They fit perfectly with the melody I had written, and . . . I learned that all I needed to write well was a topic that I care about. I realize now that the reason I had so much trouble getting started was the fact that I just hadn't found the right subject.

REVISED SELECTIONS FROM KATIE STRODE'S ANNOTATED BIBLIOGRAPHY

Annotated Bibliography

In-Depth Feature Articles

Altman, Lawrence K. "The Feud." New York Times 27 Nov. 2007.
<http://www.nytimes.com/2007/11/27/health/27docs.html?ref=science>.

> This article tells the story of a feud between two doctors that began when one doctor used an artificial heart from the lab of the other doctor in a transplant. I think it sits on the line between news and feature articles, because it tells a story and there's a lot of extra information that isn't necessarily relevant. However, it is also pretty newsworthy because the feud just ended—that's the reason the article was even written. In terms of the way it was written, I liked it a lot. It doesn't jump around or start at the end or any of that other silly journalistic stuff. It just starts at the very beginning and works its way to the present. If I end up writing an article that specifically tells a story, I think that's how I would do it.

Kantrowitz, Barbara, and Julie Scelfo. "What Happens When They Grow Up." Time 27 Nov. 2006: 47–53.

> The 'they' that the title of this article refers to is autistic adults. It's not specifically about one person, but it does refer to several different people continually throughout the article. This seems to be a common way to write a feature article that focuses on a group of people. It's fairly long, at seven pages, and includes lots of graphics, photos, and pull quotes. There is also a shorter, related article called a Figure included near the end. Including a Figure is a common thing to do with feature articles. This article was the cover story. I have a lot more to say about the craft of this article because I enjoyed reading it, which is always something to keep in mind for my article—interesting, engaging articles hold readers better than any sort of gimmick or fancy graphic. (They *do* help, though.)

Kluger, Jeffrey. "What Makes Us Moral." Time 3 Dec. 2007: 54–60.

> This article, also a cover story, is six pages long and has lots of illustrations and charts. Obviously, it's an article about what in the human brain makes us moral creatures. An interesting Figure that was included had several hypothetical situations designed to test human morality with hard situations. Figures can be interactive—it makes them more interesting. The article is written in a way that doesn't refer to the time or date, but it's probably fairly recent, given the up-to-date research that it refers to. The article could have been written two weeks ago or two months ago—it's got a longer shelf life. Like feature articles tend to be, it's a 'soft' news story. It's not about an event, but rather something that people might find interesting.

FIGURE 4.13. *Revised Selections from Katie Strode's Annotated Bibliography*

While students generally use workshop time wisely, Chelsea's familiar concern—What am I going to write about?—initially blocks some students. To light a sometimes much-needed fire under those students, Sarah holds an idea conference day early in the unit. At this conference, students are invited to either share their beginning drafts, talk through their experiences so far in the project, or float their ideas for their centerpiece with a medium-size group. On the board, Sarah writes out a protocol to use for each participant: explain your genre and what you've learned so far, ask for the help you need, share your draft or idea for your draft, receive feedback with an open mind, articulate your next steps. If possible, Sarah schedules this conference on a day when one or two preservice teachers will be visiting so that the class can divide into two or three medium-size groups, each facilitated by an adult who keeps the group on task while making sure every student has a turn and gets specific suggestions. It's important that these groups be large enough that the student who is sharing gets plenty of feedback from a variety of peers and can hear a range of students discuss an assortment of genres at various places in the process, but small enough that all students in the group will have a turn. It's also best to schedule this idea conference in plenty of time for students to complete a first draft for the scheduled due date, but close enough that there is a sense of immediacy in students' plans for next steps.

Once students settle on a topic, they spend most of their class time drafting and revising their pieces. In true workshop fashion, Sarah continues to start each class with some sort of minilesson, usually about process and craft—focusing on lessons that cross multiple genres and that arise mostly from the challenges she sees her students facing.

In the midst of this drafting and revising, a subtle shift in the atmosphere of the class often becomes apparent: students become increasingly engaged by their projects. As they move back and forth between their newfound knowledge of their genre and their ideas for the piece they're writing, they begin to see this very large undertaking come together in some exciting ways. They feel knowledgeable about their projects, proud of that knowledge, and ready to take on the challenge of revising in some authentic ways. Megan, who anticipates becoming a scientist, decided to try her hand at science articles. She explains,

> My first attempt at writing a journal article was dismal. I had created a research summary, without synthesizing the information. It was not at all close to what I had read so many of, and my audience was confused. . . . I changed how I saw the information that I was looking for in the articles I was reading. . . . After going over my very helpful notes about how the author probably went from raw information to accessible material, I tried again and got high praise.

Once students reach this point of excitement toward their chosen genre, once they are able to compose and revise their own piece that represents their best shot at writing in that genre, Sarah introduces the multiple conferences that are an essential part of the final project. Sarah requires students to confer with at least three individuals during the process: a classmate, an important adult, and her. Why three conferences? She wants students to have the experience of getting multiple responses, thinking hard about what to do with sometimes conflicting feedback, and learning how to ask for the kinds of responses that will be helpful to them as writers.

Knowing how difficult it can sometimes be for students to push themselves and their peers to offer that thoughtful and sound advice, she introduces a minilesson that teaches (or reteaches) students how to confer. Using a piece of her own writing, Sarah models what she expects of her students: she reads her piece aloud (projected on the overhead), asks for advice, and translates the students' feedback into notes she writes directly on the draft. Sarah then asks students to put on their metacognitive hats: Was this a successful conference? If so, what made it successful? Students brainstorm a list of ideas of what they noticed that led to the conference's success, focusing on behaviors from both the writer and the readers. Usually they come up with ideas like these: as the author, Sarah resisted defensiveness, she asked for what she needed, and she worked hard to understand all the suggestions; the best readers listened hard to what Sarah was trying to accomplish as a writer and offered clear and concrete suggestions. They then talk about general strategies to make their own conferences successful: ideas such as reading papers aloud and taking notes, for example, rather than just trading papers and never actually talking.

Experience has taught Sarah that as the due date for the UGP nears, she needs to make extra time for both the student-student and student-teacher conferences. Because students consistently tell her that they genuinely appreciate the one-on-one time, she offers writing conferences before school, during lunch, and after school in addition to in-class workshop time. Increasingly, Sarah builds in additional workshop days to accommodate conference requests in the two weeks before the project is due.

Sarah also asks students to practice conferring with their parents or an important adult. Although at first this seems like a risk (even though it's a required portion of the final submission), students and adults have risen to the occasion. With plenty of conference experience now behind them, students teach their parents how to confer—just as they have done in class—and in turn get suggestions from *very* interested adults. And when parents (or other adults in their lives) make time for the students and students have learned *how* to ask for useful advice, these conferences tend to be especially productive, covering ideas and content as well as craft and proofreading.

Three conferences, then, help the students with this task of revising. As they continue making changes and getting to the point of final polishing, they're ready to display their centerpiece writing: their best effort at putting into practice all they've learned about their genre.

Reflecting on the Experience

When the final draft is polished and the project is coming to a close, we want students to reflect on their experience, to articulate for themselves all they've learned. Once again, the research journal is an invaluable tool for this reflection. When students use it regularly throughout their work, each entry serves as a snapshot of the students' thinking and provides concrete evidence of growth. As students compose these reflective letters, they often cite these journals, noting that they weren't aware of how much they had changed as readers, writers, and researchers until they looked back at their first entries and remembered again their struggles with how to even get started. In the project overview, the reflective letter is described this way:

> The last piece you'll write for this project is your reflective letter. Consider your experience over the weeks of this project. Reread your journals. Reread your drafts and experimental writing. Reread your notes on your reading. With all this in mind, think about what you've learned about reading in this project. What have you learned about writing? What have you learned about studying genres and researching in general? Your reflective letter should discuss your experiences with reading, writing, your research process, and metacognition. In each of these sections, make big-picture conclusions from your experience.

Just as Sarah introduces other aspects of this project using the tools of immersion, inquiry, instruction, and integration, she shares past students' reflective letters in order to draw out of her students what might be involved in writing this genre of reflection.

"I'm going to share with you a couple of final reflective letters," Sarah starts the period.

"I was going to ask you about that. I wanted to read some examples," Austin replies.

Sarah smiles. Austin's comment lets her know that her students are incorporating these tools for genre study—especially immersion—into their thinking. "Yeah! So let's read a couple."

Sarah puts the first letter on the overhead (see Figure 4.14), and as the class discusses it, Sarah focuses students' attention on metacognition and the purpose of their reflections: "Why would I ask you to write about your metacognition in

SAMPLE REFLECTIVE LETTER BY NORMAN ZENG

I can safely say that this unfamiliar genre project has been one of the most frustrating but fulfilling one that I have ever done in my life. The project helped me push my horizons into unknown territory and helped me stimulate a new growing passion for poetry. My poetry skills were rudimentary at best before this project and I never thought that I would be able to do as well as I did. Because of this increase in growth I have gained many new opportunities that I can use in the future.

In order to write the best Haikus that I could, I did a number of things. I exchanged heavy rock music for jazz as heavy rock doesn't quite suit Haikus and went for "Haiku Walks" where I just walk to a place and watch people or nature. You notice a lot of actions that you would not have noticed otherwise when you just sit still and breathe in Mother Nature. An example, I was sitting on the bench, when a man walked by with a small white dog, who I called Spot for obvious reasons. He was sniffing everywhere and when he came next to an ant hill, I saw aunts disappearing in a flash. If I was not writing a Haiku, I would have never seen that visual imagery and furthermore, might not even notice the dog. As I was writing my Spot Haiku, I realized that writing in set syllables can be quite hard especially when the words that "flow" do not have the right sylla-bles. Sometime, you have too many syllables, and that's where free-verse comes in. It allows the Haiku writer freedom to write with as many syllables and lines he/she wants. Ultimately, I still found it more fun to write in traditional form as it has something structured, which I really like, and presents more of a challenge.

The most respected Japanese haiku masters wrote in the Japanese tradi-tional form even though a few did free-form. Through the readings of many translated books, I gathered that not only did Japances Masters write in the tradi-tional form, most of them write with a season word, usually spring floods or cherry

FIGURE 4.14. *Sample Reflective Letter by Norman Zeng*

blossoms. Researching this, I found that a season word was one of the require-ments and so was a Ki, which has no English translation, so most English haiku writers use punctuation instead even though it is not as effective. Reading was one of the easy parts of the project, the haikus of both past and present were enjoy-able and some were even so good that I had to read them multiple times. I can only strive and hope that one day I can be as good as these masters of haiku, both past and present. Even though my research was fruitful, it was not as extensive as I would have liked, I only researched parts that would help with my writing. Looking at some of the past projects of Ms. Andrew's students, I saw that they researched way more in depth than me even though that research did nothing to help the student write their genres. I stayed away from that and now I regret it as I found a couple tidbits that made me realize that the history of how Haiku was formed is a very interesting one.

In the end I realized that haikus make me look at the would in a different view, or it at least opened a different viewpoint for me, taking or using that view-point is of course up to me. Some of the best haikus throw you to the extremes of your emotional range, some make you feel happy and content, while other make you sad and realize that the world is not perfect, even if you want it to be. Throughout the project and culminating in this final reflection I realized that the Haiku is a mystical tool that has many different wonderful effects for the writer and reader. Many of these are unexplainable and can only be experienced by reading the exceptional and unique poetry form, Haiku.

Norman Zeng

> *Glance into the day—*
> *Sleepy and happy yawn*
> *Inconsequential.*
>
> *—Norman Zeng*

FIGURE 4.14. *(Continued)*

this project? Well, I want to know how you were thinking as you were learning this genre for the first time. What things were you paying attention to? What were the lightbulb moments? What were your moments of complete confusion and frustration, and how did you work your way out of those times?"

After Sarah finishes reading, she asks her students what they noticed. A female voice from the back of the room begins a series of callouts.

"It's your opinion."

"Your reflections."

"Your voice."

"Do you want us to be that casual?"

"Yes, you can be that casual. This does not have to be a formal essay. I want you to be thorough and thoughtful, of course. It's fun for me to read your voice," Sarah responds.

"Can we work on these today?"

"Yes. We'll read one more and then you can work for the rest of the period on your own reflection. Chris wrote this reflection when he was a ninth grader." Sarah begins to read sections aloud from another sample projected on the overhead: " 'The research for this project was long and frustrating.' Can anybody relate?"

"Oh yeah."

"I can."

Sarah continues reading parts of Chris' letter: " 'I don't think I could have picked many more genres that were as time consuming as this.' How many of you feel this way?"

Lots of hands go up; others smile broadly.

"You can absolutely talk about your frustrations as well as your successes," Sarah assures them. "I think you know me well enough to know that I understand that this can be frustrating, and that's OK. I want to know about your frustrations *and* how you worked through them."

"So it's OK to show our personality in our voice?" a male student wonders.

"Absolutely. It will really help you to go back and reread your research journals, which is a kind of raw data of how you were thinking, and for this reflection, you'll synthesize that into a single, informal essay, an extended research journal that sums it all up. OK? Get to work."

Student reflections continually amaze us. The students' honesty and insights about both the UGP and what they've learned as writers help us know just how valuable this teaching approach can be.

Letter from an Important Adult

When the project is compiled into a binder, complete with tabs for each section, Sarah asks her students to do one more thing before they hand in their

UGP: share their completed project with their parents or another important adult. Every teacher (and everyone who has ever parented a teenager) knows how difficult it is to keep communication flowing among parents, students, and teachers during those high school years. The 100 percent participation that was the norm for parents during curriculum nights in elementary school dwindles each year, and, as a result, it's often hard to tell if parents are clued into the ins and outs of their teens' school day.

Parents are busy; teens are busy establishing their independence from home. And yet, we know how important this communication is—both between parents and their students and between parents and teachers. Sarah has, through the UGP, found one way to keep open the conversational lines, by inviting students to ask their parents (or another adult who is important in their life) to take a moment to respond to their work. As a required part of this project, students must find an interested adult to read and respond—not to the teacher, but to the teen.

Over the years, Sarah has found this to be an invaluable part of the project. At conferences, parents have thanked her, telling her that it was the first school assignment their children had shared all year. And students are aware that they have yet one more audience for the project.

Sarah introduces this part of the assignment in this way: "Today we're going to talk about one kind of response to the UGP, a letter from an important adult—a parent, an older sibling, your neighbor, anyone whom you are close to or you would like to share your hard work with. After the person reads your work, I want you to ask this person to write a letter *to you* about what he or she noticed in your project. This is not a letter to me. I do not want your parents to write me, saying, 'Ms. Andrew, my student deserves an A because. . . .' Rather, this is a chance for someone who is important to you to sit down, look at your project, and respond to the hard work you are doing in this class."

As Sarah continues with the introduction, she explains to the students that she is aware that asking parents to read their work might be a little unusual and even uncomfortable for them. She explains, "I get that it's good that your parents don't have to look over your shoulder and make sure that you are doing your homework, but it's nice for them to get a sense of what you're doing at school. As a parent, I like to know what my kids are doing at school." And she assures them that they don't need to worry that their parents' writing isn't good enough. She says, "I've had parents write in their home language to their child, and that's fine. It doesn't matter because it's not to me; it's to you, the student, and whatever words they choose, those are the right words for that audience!"

The letters don't need to be fancy. Sarah shares one from a parent, pointing out that it's not formal, not revised, just a letter from parent to teen. Some parents type them up, but more often they're on lined paper, written in pencil or pen. (See Figure 4.15 for one parent's letter.)

PARENT LETTER TO A STUDENT
WHO STUDIED SHORT STORIES

Dear _____,

Thank you for sharing your English project with me. I always appreciate any opportunity that helps me to know you better. I think writing, by its very nature, is one of the best forms of communication. Unlike spontaneous conversation, it tends to be more thoughtful and purposeful. I'm assuming this was the case when you wrote "Dual Dance." So, you can only imagine my ambivalence when I read this piece of writing.

_____, you are a good writer! You say it is hard for you—I know you prefer to read—but your efforts certainly pay off. I was immediately caught up in the story—you had my undivided attention by the third line. And, then, you held my interest throughout the entire story. I couldn't wait to see how it ended. Of course, I was horrified by it. How awful that this child should die.

As a mother, this story raises all kinds of red flags. My gut response was to believe that this is somewhat autobiographical. I had to fight the urge to start paging through the yellow pages in search of a good counselor. I don't know, _____, I sense a lot of underlying anger and hurt in this character. Maybe we have some ongoing issues that we haven't resolved. Maybe this is purely fiction and I am over-reacting. I need you to help me figure it out.

My other thought is that Ms. Andrew is a wonderful teacher. When I went to school—back in the dark ages, before they had discovered the printing press—my teacher would not have accepted this work. I would have to have written a traditional short story, well developed in every way, to have completed the assignment. I also would have been asked to read a collection of famous authors—certainly not anything as contemporary as what you've read. I'm glad you've had the chance to explore these current authors. I know you're capable of understanding and discussing all those other "high brow" types as well.

I will look forward to some kind of follow up discussion about your project. Thanks for including me on this.
Mom

May be copied for classroom use. © 2009 by Cathy Fleischer and Sarah Andrew-Vaughan from Writing Outside Your Comfort Zone *(Heinemann: Portsmouth, NH).*

FIGURE 4.15. *Parent Letter to a Student Who Studied Short Stories*

Assessment

The success of projects like the UGP depends on multiple assessments along the way, both formal and informal. Daily in class, Sarah conducts check-ins with the students, asking them to show her their progress on gathering and annotating their samples, keeping up with their how-to books, drafting and revising their genre exemplars. Sometimes these check-ins take the form of a simple question ("How's it going today? Who had a success or a challenge?"), sometimes Sarah literally checks students off in her grade book, and often students share their progress in the form of whole-class or one-on-one conferences. Vital to the assessment process, these check-ins serve a dual purpose: first, they help keep students on track and moving along, a necessary component of a project that is this big and in which each step builds upon the last. Most students, despite some good-natured grumbles, understand and appreciate the importance of these along-the-way deadlines: clear expectations and a clear time frame ease the fears of taking on such a big and unfamiliar project. That said, anticipate that not all students will be prepared for every check, which leads to an equally important reason for these check-ins: the information they offer us as teachers, letting us know how students are doing and what challenges are confronting them as they work through the multiple components. We might learn through these informal assessments that the whole class is struggling with a particular component or idea, letting us know it's time to revise a lesson plan, circle back to reiterate a section, rethink how to reach students who are confused. Or, as is more often the case, some individual students might be struggling with a particular part, and the check lets us hone in on the problem and work one-on-one to get the students over the hump. We believe any project of this depth and breadth almost *requires* this kind of ongoing check-in in order to take the pulse of both individual students and the class as a whole and drive the kind and pace of instruction. (Another hint: For those students who just can't seem to make headway in their projects, Sarah sometimes announces at the beginning of a workshop day that a check that will occur at the end of that period; she finds this quick deadline ensures a productive workshop.)

This formative assessment is consistently integrated into the daily class structure of this assignment and is an invaluable means for us to see where our students are in the process. The second prong of our assessment, though, is summative in nature: a way of letting the students know at the end of the project just how well they've done. This summative assessment is based on the entire research binder the students produce over the course of the project, a binder that includes their final draft of original writing in the studied genre, their reflective letter about the project, their how-to book, the drafts in progress, their annotated bibliography, and their research journal. Early on in the project, Sarah gives the students the broad rubric she uses (shown in Figure 4.16),

UNFAMILIAR GENRE PROJECT RUBRIC

Author's Checklist	A 9–10 points	B 8 points	C 7 points	D 6 points	E 0–5 points
Reflective letter (discusses your reading, writing, metacognition, and research)	insightful	perceptive	observant	somewhat reflective	none
Final piece looks and reads like stated genre	excellent	good job	average	little effort	doesn't look or read like genre
Final piece is readable, interesting, engaging, and enjoyable	excellent	good job	average	little effort	poorly written
Research journal is thorough (Write an entry each time you work on the project.)	12 or more	9–11 entries	6–8 entries	3–5 entries	0–2 entries
Research journal explains your research process, metacognition, and experience	insightful	perceptive	process addressed	somewhat addressed	none
All drafts and experiments	plentiful	ample	sufficient	few	none
Conference notes (from parents, peers, and teacher; label each on own draft)	plentiful	ample	sufficient	few	none
Collection of five to ten published samples in MLA style	good choices	representative	adequate	poor choices	none
Annotation for each sample	insightful	perceptive	observant	somewhat reflective	none
Proofreading (final piece, reflective letter, annotated bibliography)	very few errors	some errors	same errors throughout	many errors	excessive errors

Notes:

FIGURE 4.16. Parent Letter to a Student Who Studied Short Stories

explaining to students that each of the ten categories will be worth 10 percent of the rubric grade.

The rubric begins with consideration of the students' reflective letter, which asks them to evaluate their progress and learning through the unit. The next two categories credit students for their final draft of the genre they have chosen, focusing both on how much their version fits the genre and how successful it is as an actual piece of writing that would be "interesting, engaging, and enjoyable" to a reader. Another 20 percent goes to the research journal: for regularly and consistently writing their entries and for demonstrating thoughtful metacognition in the entries. The rubric also honors the students' progress, as Sarah looks at their experiments, drafts, and conference notes. The annotated bibliography, a huge part of the project, is weighted heavily with another 20 percent: both the inclusion of sufficient samples and thoughtful annotations of the samples. Finally, Sarah emphasizes the importance of presentation in this large project with the last category of proofreading. Specifically, she expects the final drafts of their genre, reflection, and annotated bibliography to be polished and proofread.

This clearly defined and easy-to-use rubric provides students, parents, and even counselors with a fairly clear picture of how the students have done on the project; all these groups can easily look over the circles to see where the students excelled and where they came up short. However, we recognize that rubrics alone can go only so far in representing any student's growth and learning for any particular project (see, for example, Maja Wilson's *Rethinking Rubrics in Writing Assessment* [2006]). Rubrics, no matter how well designed and thoughtful, measure only the teacher's preconceived categories, failing to note the individual growth and often nuanced learning that students gain. Rubrics, in other words, reflect certain qualities, but not everything.

Both of us have struggled with the place of rubrics in our teaching, recognizing their value, but feeling they are not quite enough. Over the past few years, Sarah's rubric has changed in various ways as she's worked to make it represent more accurately her objectives in the UGP and the qualities of the work the students produce. More recently, though, she's moved to a two-tiered approach to final assessment for this project: 50 percent based on the rubric and 50 percent based on the growth and progress students have shown as readers and writers. This second part of the assessment is reflected in an individual letter Sarah composes for each student based on her overall reading of the binder and her notes on the student's participation and performance in the project. (See Figure 4.17 for a sample letter.)

These letters, Sarah admits, *do* take a lot of time. But, as she explains, students need, want, and deserve much more response than mere circles on a chart, especially after the work they've put in on this project. In these letters,

Taylor,

Your hard work on this project certainly *does* show throughout. In fact, you are one of the most passionate, hardworking "productive procrastinators" I know! I love that you really do research and follow your nose into the topics (and ideas) that interest you. This is really valuable: you know how to—and enjoy—research.

And you are self-aware. You practically write your whole piece in your mind, start over, edit, rewrite, edit again—still in your mind—and then finally put pen to paper, all the while feeling like you aren't doing what you're supposed to. The truth: We don't all follow the same, prescribed process. We aren't assembly lines, and neither is research. Further, we don't all work "efficiently." That isn't to say that it's OK to put off work, but it is OK to have your own process, so long as it actually *works* for you. Another truth: my process isn't all that different from yours.

Here's what I've learned about writing this way: we have to learn to accept the way we are and work with it, which, for writing, means that we need to give ourselves plenty of time to think about the project within the deadlines set for us. The key here is to *not* procrastinate starting, because I know I can safely say that we both know the value of conferences and the "tiny" revisions that take our writing from *good* to *really good*. One more truth: like you, I'm still working on this and I imagine I always will. The key, I think, is to be self-aware, and you've come a long way in this.

So, I'm proud of you for finishing this large project on time despite this fluid, time-consuming process. I've seen you learning *how* to come in on deadline this year. Hurray!

And of course I love your children's story! Every child I've known has experienced feeling afraid at bedtime. I think it's clever how you combined the big brother's antics with the child's perception of the monster—I've seen my own kids combine reality with their imaginations.

Bravo, Taylor! You've written and illustrated a beautiful, compelling picture book. What an accomplishment. Will you write another? Will you consider publishing this book; perhaps you might laminate it and give it to a young friend or donate it to the library?

Yours in following our noses,

Ms. Andrew

Figure 4.17. *Sample Teacher Response Letter*

Sarah has a chance to note each student's growth, celebrate accomplishments, and make suggestions for future growth.

Lessons Learned

In this chapter, we've tried to give you some very hands-on suggestions for incorporating the Unfamiliar Genre Project at the high school level, based on work with a number of classes over a number of years. The next chapter offers you a sample UGP from one student, something you can use as a model for the students in your class (to give them a sense of what a completed one might encompass) or just to help you envision what the finished product might be. And in Chapter 5, we share some variations we've put into practice in a journalism class, in a literature class, and in a methods class at the college level.

What have we learned from our work with the UGP, using it regularly in our classes for five years? Most obvious to us is the potential it offers students: the breadth and depth of the work they voluntarily undertake in this project is stunning. Students choose genres as varied as microfiction, scrapbook, sonnet, political pamphlet, and novel. And it doesn't end there. Students report that within the short weeks of the project, they are amazed by the dramatic changes they see in their learning. Leo, who studied cookbooks, said,

> This project helped me a lot more than I expected it to. I thought this was just going to be like any other project, but it was different from most of the ones that I have done before. . . . The project has opened my eyes to new forms of writing and has shown me how the format and aspects of writing make the piece. . . . As a reader, I will now pay more attention to different formats and styles of writing so I can incorporate them into my own. . . . I found myself just today reading my dad's newspaper and paying attention to the special way it was written.

What's more, students internalize their newfound skills and feel empowered to put them to work. Susan, who investigated instruction manuals, explained,

> My writing benefited from having to pay such close attention to detail. . . . This was a change for me because I am used to writing where detail and specifics are not so important. It helped me develop some discipline. . . . I will never read a book or any other piece of written material quite the same again. This project taught me to look for the specific qualities that make each genre unique. I now read as if I am on a treasure hunt, and I am searching for clues. . . . I have a brand new perspective on reading, one that I probably would not have learned without having done this project.

Holly wrote,

When we were first told about this project, I immediately thought, 'PHOTO-JOURNALISM!' I figured that it would be an interesting genre for me to study because I love seeing the news through pictures, and I like to take pictures myself. And, yes, I will admit, I also thought it would be an easy genre to study. I figured by taking a few pictures I would be excused from the researching and revising that writing an actual article requires. Sadly, I was wrong. Photojournalism turned out to be much more complicated than I expected. . . . Although I did get frustrated every now and then, I learned a lot from this project. I think the biggest lesson I learned was that to do something well, time and hard work must be applied, no matter how easy the task may seem.

Much as we love these student endorsements, we'd be remiss if we didn't talk at least briefly about the frustration Holly (and many other students over the years) mentioned. This project is *hard*: hard for students and hard for teachers, and there is often a point partway through the project when all of us wonder if the end result will be worth it. Our advice to you as a teacher trying this for the first time is this: Hang in there with it! Recognize, acknowledge, affirm your students' fears and frustrations. This is a *real* part of writers' processes. If teachers can see their way to validating these frustrations, it helps the students stay on track; help them look at the big picture, and—most of all—try to have fun. We think the end results are worth it.

The students, actually, have convinced us that this project is a worthwhile and welcome addition to their ways of learning. They learn some traditional research skills—how to use the library, how to use the Internet, and how to critically assess and annotate their findings—and have the added benefit of applying those skills in an immediate and tangible fashion. The long-range benefits are important as well: as students learn more about the concept of genre, they are more informed readers and writers, understanding in a real way that various genres have various demands and using that awareness to approach the new as well as the familiar genres they encounter. Further, researching their genre helps students gain confidence that they can take on new writing tasks—a tangible end to the sometimes elusive research unit. And, if you're thinking that perhaps this project is most useful with successful writers, we've found that even the least confident writers grow in very tangible ways over the course of the project. Will their final projects be as full and presented as beautifully as some of their more confident peers? Not in all cases, but what many have produced has really taken our breath away.

Julia, whose final UGP you'll read in the next chapter, is an interesting example of this: she began the class without much confidence in her ability as a writer, but created one of the strongest UGPs in her class. From the first, she was intriguing: black nail polish, bobbed hair, strong sense of personal style. She walked into the classroom on that first day directly to the seat of her choice—in the farthest back corner of the room. Her presence was loud, but her voice quiet, both because she didn't speak up often in class and because she didn't *project*. Yet what most distinguished Julia was the quality of her work. She quickly set herself apart as a talented artist, drawing with perspective and detail unmatched by most of her peers. Her writing assignments demonstrated the same kind of detail and thoughtfulness. At the end of the first-quarter conference, Sarah told her how impressed she was with her work and wondered if she was planning to study writing in college. Julia was shocked by the suggestion. Her? A writer? She'd never seen herself that way.

We surely did. And after you have the chance to read Julia's music review, reflection on her learning, and the component parts that led to these writings in Chapter 5, we think you will, too.

5

Learning by Example

A Sample UGP

THROUGHOUT THIS BOOK, we've emphasized the importance of immersing students in samples of the genre under discussion and inquiring into those samples, whether it's author blurb, comic book, annotated bibliography, or reflective letter. That same approach works well for the final binder for the UGP. When students get a chance to see samples of the finished binders their peers have produced over the years, they both breathe a sigh of relief (students *do* finish these projects!) and see the vast array of genres and approaches to the genres created by other students their own age. We often do a museum walk with these samples: placing them on a table or desk and inviting students to browse through them, paper and pen in hand, as they note what seems interesting, unusual, or appealing about the projects. We then discuss together which ones they liked and why.

Because you won't have this array of sample projects the first time you teach the UGP, we offer you here one complete project, to be used alongside the various sample components we included in Chapter 4. This example comes from Julia Rosenzweig, whom we described briefly in the last chapter and who was a junior when she studied concert reviews as her unfamiliar genre.

We include Julia's sample here both because it is well done and because it represents a strong example of the kind of product we generally receive. And while we include it as part of this teacher-oriented book, so that you can envision what a final product might look like, we also encourage you to share this example with your students. You might ask them to inquire into it, talking about what they notice, what they like and don't like, what they might take from this when they produce their own UGP. And because we believe that immersion works best when multiple products are part of that immersion, we invite you to view even more samples by visiting the link to this book on the Heinemann website.

For more examples of Unfamiliar Genre Projects, visit our website, heinemann.com/books/unfamiliar.

These samples, of course, cannot substitute for the concrete, physical binders that your students will begin producing and that you will then have to share with future students, so we encourage you to start gathering samples of your own students' writing from the very beginning of your journey into the UGP. The bigger variety of genres you can collect, the better for the students. But in the meantime, enjoy Julia's!

Julia's Unfamiliar Genre Project: Concert Review

1. Reflective Letter

2. UGP Proposal

3. Genre Scavenger Hunt

4. Final Centerpiece Music Review

5. Research Journal

6. Conference Notes

7. Annotated Bibliography

8. How-to Book

9. Letter from an Interested Adult

10. Assessment: Letter and Rubric

Reflective Letter

This semester, more than anything else, I have learned about myself as a writer. I've always known that I have a tendency to write at the last minute, but I just figured it was because I was procrastinating. While this may be true sometimes, I've learned that

I actually do write better later at night. I also learned that it takes me a really long time to write. These two factors combined make for some very late nights with not much sleep. Before this year, I would get very frustrated with this. But now I've come to terms with the fact that the quality of my writing is noticeably better when I take my time with it and work when I feel most creative. Now I know that sometimes sacrificing a few hours of sleep is worth it, as long as I can write well.

Through this project especially, I've learned that it's much better to write about something you care about. The topic I chose for this project is something that's very important to me, and I knew it was absolutely necessary to do it justice. I pushed myself a lot harder with this project, and worked on it almost every day for three weeks straight, which is something I never do. I learned how important it is to feel connected to what you're writing about, because the quality suffers when you don't care what you're writing about.

Through doing this project, I also learned how to be a more comprehensive reader. Because I was required to read so much, I decided I might as well try to enjoy it and actually gain something from it, which I definitely did. I tried to learn something from each sample that I read, but I don't think I learned much about reading in general.

The research process involved with this project was very extensive, but really beneficial and helpful. Reading the different samples of my genre definitely influenced me a lot. If I hadn't been so immersed in reading my genre, I probably would've been really lost about what to write and how to write it. This kind of process I'm sure will help me a lot in the future.

My main challenge with this project was projecting the right kind of voice. Most writers in this genre use the first-person perspective, but still sound professional. Usually when I write in the first-person perspective, I tend to sound really unprofessional and immature, so I had to think a lot about how I wanted my voice to sound. I wanted to sound laid back, but not too casual. I wanted to sound authoritative, but not stiff. With every sentence I wrote, I had to stop and think about whether or not it projected the voice I was hoping for. Metacognition helped me be a more meticulous writer, because I was constantly stopping myself to make sure I was going in the right direction.

Genre Project Proposal

Which genre would you like to read and write in for your Unfamiliar Genre Project?
    Concert review/profile

What experiences, if any, do you have with reading or writing in this genre?
    None with writing. I've only read reviews sent to me by other people because they're bad.

What do you already know about this genre?
    Not that much.

Why are you choosing this genre?

Because it's something I care a lot about and I think I will do a better job on it since I want to do it justice.

What would you like to learn by studying this genre and completing this project?

How to write positively about something while being unbiased.

Genre Scavenger Hunt

1. **What's your genre? (Does it go by any other names?)**
   Review—concert

2. **Who are some famous or well-known authors/writers of your genre?**
   Jason Tate, Drew Beringer

3. **Where might you find information on the Internet about your genre?**
   Wikipedia, newspaper website, absolutepunk.net

4. **What key words or phrases might you type into a search engine to find samples of your genre?**
   Concert Review

5. **How and where might you find instructions for how to write in your genre on the Internet?**
   Bookstore, how-to section

6. **Where in the library might you look for samples of your genre?**
   News archives

7. **Where in the library might you find instructional materials for how to write in your genre?**
   How-to section

8. **If you don't know where to find information in the library, whom or where might you ask for help?**
   The librarian

9. **Is there any other place (bookstore, television, parent's office, etc.) where you could find samples of your genre? Where?**
   Newspaper, Internet, television

10. **Is there any other place (local newspaper, parent's office, teacher, etc.) where you could find help writing in your genre?**
    Bookstore

11. **Who are some local authors/writers of your genre? (Name as many as you can.)**
    Nathan Lint, James Parker (photographer)

Spitalfield Says "Goodbye" with Curtain Call Tour

Story and photos by Julia Rosenzweig

"Dearest fans & friends. After nine years, nine countries, over a thousand shows and more than a lifetime worth of memories, it comes with a heavy heart that Spitalfield will be calling it quits. This choice has been one of the hardest things any of us have ever gone through, as the decision has absolutely nothing to do with the lack of passion for making music together or love for each other."

Upon reading the statement posted on Spitalfield's Myspace in September, I found myself short of breath. These were the words I had been expecting, yet totally dreading, to read for quite some time. Spitalfield has been one of my absolute favorite bands since 2005, and hearing that they were splitting up was heartbreaking. But, lucky for me,

not only were they going to do one last tour, they booked two dates within an hour of me - one in Toledo, the other in Detroit. Knowing this would be my last chance to see them, I decided I had to go to both shows.

The first show was on Friday, November 30th at Headliner's in Toledo, Ohio. I've been fortunate enough to see Spitalfield play four different times in the past couple of years, and every time they were nothing short of amazing. My expectations for this show were ridiculously high because of that, and I definitely wasn't let down.

After waiting outside in line for about 45 minutes (it was REALLY cold, by the way), we were finally let inside the

venue. The first band to play was The Welcoming Committee, though the label "band" is misleading, because The Welcoming Committee is just a 20-year-old guy who plays acoustic guitar and sings (badly). I was not impressed by his set in the least, but he did play a nice cover of Jimmy Eat World's "Kill".

Up next was Plague the City, a rock/pop group from Toledo. Although their music was somewhat mediocre, they performed with lots of energy, which made their set much more enjoyable. The rest of the crowd seemed to be really into them too, judging by the crowdsurfers and decent-sized mosh pits. They ended their last song with a bang, when Blake (vocalist) decided to hang upside-down from the ceil-

ing over the crowd. This was pretty awkward for me though, considering that I was directly underneath him.

The next band to play was Attention, fronted by former Gratitude guitarist Jeremy Tappero. I thought Attention was pretty talented - I liked all of their songs, they obviously knew how to play their instruments, but they just weren't very exciting. For a band named Attention, they didn't do a very good job of keeping the crowd's attention. I noticed the girl next to me was texting through their whole set, and I don't blame her. They were pretty dull.

The Graduate was next, and they were a breath of fresh air. After having to stand through three mediocre bands, I was excited to finally see a band that was not only talented musically, but was also entertaining live. They're one of those bands I could see hundreds of times and never get bored with, even though they've played pretty much the same set every time I've seen them. However this time, they changed everything around completely. I noticed that vocalist Corey

Spitalfield plays Toledo one last time.

Warning seemed to be in somewhat of a bad mood, which was a bit disheartening. Nevertheless, they played very well and sounded spot-on. They finished their set with a song called "The Formula." Complete with gang vocals and a drum-off at the end, it was one of the highlights of the night. The crowd really loved them, and based on the reactions of the people around me, they gained quite a few new fans.

After The Graduate's performance, the night went from exciting to really, really boring thanks to The Forecast. I'm usually not a fan of bands with female vocalists, and The Forecast is no exception. Instead of singing, vocalist/bassist Shannon Burns screeches and howls. I could tolerate it for about their first four songs, but once the fifth song hit I was about ready to kill myself. Not only does Burns have a horrendous voice, but all their songs sound exactly the same, mak-

ing them boring and monotonous as well as painful to listen to. The only reason I bothered staying for them was because there was no way I was going to give up my spot on the barricade, knowing that Spitalfield was next.

Once The Forecast finished playing, I had a rush of a strange mix of emotions. I was excited to see Spitalfield, but on the flipside, I almost didn't want to see them play. It was hard knowing that after the show that night, I'd only get to see them one more time and that was it. But the second they started playing, I forgot all about being sad about about them breaking up. This is the reason I love this band so much - they make me forget about everything, and they've never failed to make me happy when I've been upset.

They opened with the first song I'd ever heard by them, "Those Days You

Felt Alive," which is off their first album *Remember Right Now*. The rest of their set was a mix of songs that spanned their entire career. They played a few songs they'd never played live before, such as "In the Same Lifetime" and "Hold On". They played a bunch of old favorites that they hadn't played in years, like "Maybe Someday" and "Make My Heart Attack."

This was by far the best I'd ever seen Spitalfield play, and they got a better crowd response than I'd ever seen. Everyone there was dancing, singing along, and having a great time. A few friends of the band even came on stage to sing during a couple of songs. Near the end of the set, it was obvious that a lot of people were getting emotional. Between songs, singer/guitarist Mark Rose mentioned that they had played at Headliner's more than anywhere else in the United States, except for their hometown of Chicago. Toledo provide to be a very loyal second home, seeing as many friends and long time fans came

onstage to sing backup vocals throughout the night.

They finished the set with "I Loved the Way She Said L.A.," easily their most popular and well-known song. Everyone in the crowd went wild, and chanted for an encore for a long time after the song ended. Sadly, Spitalfield was done for the night, leaving everyone hungry for more.

Nine days after the show in Toledo, it was time for Spitalfield's last show in Detroit, which was also the last night of the Curtain Call Tour. Over 200 people braved the crappy driving conditions (sleet, freezing rain . . . bad) to make it out to the Magic Stick. Their fanbase may be small, but incredibly dedicated nonetheless.

I met up with my friend Dan about an hour before doors were supposed to open for a couple rounds of bowling.

Fireworks is a very promising act, I'm expecting great things from them in the future.

The Magic Stick is upstairs, over a café and bowling alley. The best thing about this is that you don't have to wait in line outside in the cold for most shows. After countless shows where I've had to wait outside in below freezing temperatures for hours, it's always a nice break to come to the Magic Stick.

They let us upstairs about 15 minutes after the doors were supposed to open, and Dan and I secured a spot right in front. There was no barricade, so we sat on the stage between bands. The laid back atmosphere is another thing I love about this venue. I actually think it's one of my favorites now.

The first band to play was Fireworks, a local group from the metro Detroit area. I've heard good things about them for a while now, and I was excited to see them. They were very energetic and joked around a lot between songs. Their front-

man told the crowd a funny story about how he got fired from his job at Starbucks for throwing coffee at Red Wings caption Steve Yzerman. I was also surprised at how talented they were - the bassist didn't even have fingers on his right hand! Fireworks is a very promising act, I'm expecting great things from them in the future.

After the disappointing set from Attention in Toledo, I was anticipating another dull set from them. I couldn't have been more wrong. This time, they were much more engaging and they sounded a lot better. I was baffled at how much they had improved, wondering how it was possible that they were so boring the last time but so great this time. And then Jeremy (vocalist/ guitar) mentioned between songs that this was only their 14th show - EVER. Their improvement started making

The Graduate took the stage next . . . and blew me away.

more sense after I found out that little bit of information. If they can get so much better after only one week, I would love to see how much better they are in a few months or years.

The Graduate took the stage next. For this being my seventh time seeing them in less than a year (my personal record), I probably shouldn't have expected any surprises from them. But, as usual, they completely went against my expectations and blew me away. For one thing, they all came out wearing interesting headgear - Tom Cruise circa *Risky Business* sunglasses, bandanas, a bright green poker visor, etc. It was pretty funny, considering I've never seen them have such a sense of humor about themselves before.

The Forecast . . . were still painful to listen to. . . .

Since they left "Interlude" and "Doppelganger" out of their set on Friday, I was assuming they wouldn't play them this time around either. They usually play these two songs, and I was bummed when they changed their normal set around. It was a nice surprise when they ended up playing both. Corey also seemed to be in a much better mood than he was in Toledo, and it definitely made a difference in the intensity of their performance. They ended with their trademark drum-off during "The Formula," which is still the most impressive part of their set.

For as much as Attention had improved since the week before, The Forecast should've done the same, right? Wrong. They were still painful to listen to, Shannon's vocals still made my ears bleed, and I was still bored with their whole performance. The only thing that kept me from falling asleep this time was Dan sarcastically pretending to love them, which had me cracking up. Once again, I was relieved when they were done playing.

Spitalfield played pretty much the same songs as they did in Toledo, but it was still a really great set. They played an even mix of materials from all of their albums again. Though there was nothing really new and exciting about what they played, it didn't matter because they put their hearts and souls into their performance. That's more important to me anyway. They played most of my favorites, including "Texa$ with a Dollar Sign," "Simple Minds," "Simple Lives," and "Gold Dust vs. the State of Illinois." They were nothing short of fantastic.

Really, the only negative I can say about Spitalfield that night was the fight that broke out in the middle of "In the Same Lifetime." Some drunk idiot (who was obviously only there for the bar in the back of the venue)

kept shouting out the names of random songs that had nothing to do with Spitalfield. He went past the obligatory request for "Freebird" and started yelling for random 90's alt-rock ballads ("The Freshmen" by The Verve Pipe, anyone?) Every time he requested a different song, the people around him would tell him to shut up. This went on for about twenty minutes, until someone got fed up and knocked him out. The drunk guy got kicked out, and the night went back to normal.

Spitalfield closed with "I Loved the Way She Said L.A." Though it was one of their last shows ever, and my last time seeing them, the overall mood of the room was very upbeat and fun. It was more like a party than a funeral, and it was a great way to say goodbye.

After the show, I had the chance to talk to Mark of Spitalfield for a bit. He was more than willing to even talk to one of my friends who couldn't make it to the show on the phone. He's definitely

one of the nicest and genuine people I've met, and luckily, I should be seeing him again someday soon.

"I'm definitely not done making music. The rest of the band, not so much. I'm a '24-years-young' kind of guy. . . . I've got more, I promise," Mark said when asked about his future as a musician.

All in all, though the fact that Spitalfield is done is pretty heartbreaking, I'm glad I was able to see them a few times. And I'll always have their music, which is what matters most, right? I certainly hope so.

For larger and color versions of the photos in this article, please visit www.flickr.com/photos/fallwayaway/

You can listen to Spitalfield, as well as find links to the rest of the bands in this review, on their Myspace at http://www.myspace.com/spitalfield

Research Journal

11/27/07

Today I worked on my bibliography. I finished citing seven out of ten different sources. Something I noticed is that the bibliography websites made it a lot easier and faster to get work done. If I had to do all the work by hand, I wouldn't be nearly as close to being done as I am now. While reading different articles, I noticed that the reviewers tended to write in the first-person point of view and added a lot of their own experience to their review.

11/29/07

Today, we worked on our how-to booklets. We discussed audience and purpose, which made me think a lot more about why I was writing this article and who I was writing it for. I think now I'll be more involved in this process because now I'll be writing for more reasons than just to finish the assignment.

11/30/07

Honestly, I did not get much work done today. I was distracted by the upcoming weekend and it was hard to concentrate. I did brainstorm a bit about what I was going to write, though.

12/4/07

We worked on our how-to booklets again today. This time, the discussion was on organization, presentation, voice, and word choice. I hadn't given much thought to any of those things regarding my article yet so it was definitely an eye-opener. I realized that I tend to either write for adults and teachers and sound overly professional, or if I'm writing for my friends I pay no attention to grammar or spelling. I think it'll be hard to find a balance between the two for this article, since I want to write for people my age but still sound professional.

12/5/07

Tonight while I was working on writing my draft, I realized I'm kind of worried about writing a review that does Spitalfield justice. They've been incredibly important to me for the past couple of years, and I want to be able to write something that accurately portrays that. I think it might be harder for me to write something that I care so much about because it's causing me to be overly critical of myself.

12/6/07

Today in class, I brought in the first draft of my review. I didn't get much feedback on it yet, I think I'll wait till I've completely finished my draft to ask people to review it. I don't think it makes much sense to ask for feedback when my work isn't completed, because then I'll just have to ask for more help later.

12/10/07

Last night, I went to the second show that I'm writing about for this review. It was a great experience, and it gave me a ton to write about. Most of the bands played a lot better than they did at the first show, so I'll be able to write about that. I also took a few decent pictures that I'm excited to use in my piece.

12/11/07

Today in class, we learned how to write annotated bibliographies. I thought it was pretty helpful. By reading my samples comprehensively I gained a lot of insight about what to include in my piece. It's definitely helping a lot to have references to look back on when I get stuck or confused about what to write.

12/12/07

I wrote my first annotated bibliography in class today. It was a little more difficult than I expected; I was assuming I just had to write what perspective it's written in and other arbitrary details. I was obviously wrong about that—it takes a lot of focusing on the actual content of a sample to understand it completely and to write a good annotation.

12/13/07

Since I finished my annotated bibliography last night, I worked on my actual draft today. I added a couple pictures and edited what I already had written so far. In the next week, I need to work a lot on finishing my draft, considering that I only have half of it written out so far. I'm not worried about getting it done though, I have a pretty solid grasp on what I'm going to write. I just need to budget my time well so I don't end up putting it off till the last minute.

12/19/07

In class, we were given time to ask for peer conferencing. Once again, I chose not to do this and I opted to work on my draft instead. I work a lot better in a school setting, rather than at home where I get distracted too easily. I got a significant amount of writing done, but I still have a lot to do tonight.

12/19/07

I finished my first draft tonight! I've emailed it to a few of my friends for peer editing/conferencing, including someone who is the editor of her school paper. I really value her opinion on journalism and writing in general, so I'm excited to see what she has to say about it. Tonight, I need to edit and finish my centerpiece, write a reflection, have my mom write my letter, and organize everything. I'm glad that I don't have too much work to do tomorrow night, it's saving me a lot of stress.

Conference Notes on Drafts (from Three Peer Reviewers)

Reviewer 1

> Dearest fans & friends,
>
> After nine years, nine countries, over a thousand shows and more than a lifetime worth of memories, it comes with a heavy heart that Spitalfield will be calling it quits. This choice has been one of the hardest things any of us have ever gone through, as the decision has absolutely nothing to do with a lack of passion for making music together or love for each other.

Good opener. Instantly pulls people in and gets their attention. It makes them want to read more and find out what's going on.

> I noticed the girl next to me was texting through their whole set, and I don't blame her. They were pretty dull.

Maybe add more detail in the last sentence or at least substitute "dull" with another adjective like mind-numbing, etc. to pull people back in and conclude the paragraph in a better way.

> The laid back atmosphere is another thing I love about this venue; I actually think it's one of my favorites now.

I just changed the comma to a semicolon, just a grammar thing.

> They were very energetic and joked around a lot between songs. Their frontman told the crowd a funny story about how he got fired from his job at Starbucks for throwing coffee at Red Wings captain Steve Yzerman. I was also surprised at how talented they were—the bassist didn't even have fingers on his right hand!

Good thing to add, make people interested and laugh which is always important.

> This is the reason I love this band so much—they make me forget about everything, and they've never failed to make me happy when I've been upset.

I think it's good to give it a little personal touch. It helps people relate to the story more and in this case, picture a band that might do the same thing for them.

> "I'm definitely not done making music . . . ." Mark said when asked about his future as a musician.

A quote from the band guy is really good for a review—lets the readers see a little about who this guy is.

Reviewer 2

> and hearing that they were breaking up was heartbreaking

The word choice here is kind of redundant. Replace "breaking up" with "splitting" maybe?

> But, lucky for me, not only were they going to do one last tour, **but** they booked two dates within an hour of me

Eliminate the bold. It's redundant.

> (it was REALLY cold, by the way)

Haha. I like that. It gives the story a more personal feel.

> The crowd really loved them, and they gained many new fans.

Do you know for sure that they gained many new fans?

As far as the article as a review goes, I think there's still room for improvement. While your opinions were good, they should sound less like opinions and more like assertions. For example, instead of saying things like, "They were really energetic, and although I don't really care for their music, I enjoyed their set," you could rephrase it to say something like, "Although their music was only mediocre, their energy made the set enjoyable." First person is used too abundantly throughout the story, which makes it sound more like a blog than an article.

Technicalities aside, the article had terrific voice and a distinct style, which makes it more personal, relatable, and a really enjoyable read overall. For such a long article, it definitely held my attention throughout. Good job!

Reviewer 3

First thing: I'd watch your diction in some spots. i.e., would you really describe it as an "emphasis" of lyrics, vocals, etc? (I think you should keep it succinct by saying "stop doing bad things is the perfect balance of . . .") and "messed up" kind of disrupts the tone (I would try "corrupt").

Also, I'd be careful of your arrangement of sentences in some places. For example, you talk about how Spitalfield is forced to break up, then you say, "Van Buren" describes the "messy situation" which implies that the song was written about their break up.

Otherwise, you did a really thorough job and you definitely gave a comprehensive summary of what they sound like. Good job.

Annotated Bibliography

1. Haas, Hugo. "The Smashing Pumpkins @ The Fillmore—2007-07-28." <u>Hugo's Blog</u>. 30 July 2007. <u>Google</u>. 27 Nov. 2007 <http://larve.net/people/hugo/2005/blog/2007/07/30/the-smashing-pumpkins-the-fillmore-2007-07-28/>.

This review was really helpful to me. The writer included his personal experience at the concert and wrote in the first person point of view. He included a lot of details about The Smashing Pumpkins, including what they had done before their current tour, their setlist, and how well they played. What I didn't like was that he didn't say enough about the opening band—he didn't even mention their name. This review was helpful because at first I wasn't sure what to include, and this was a good guide.

2. Williams, Alun. "The Who—Concert Review." <u>About.com: Classic Rock</u>. 29 Sep. 2006. About.com. Google. 27 Nov. 2007 <http://classicrock.about.com/od/artistsnz/fr/who_concert.htm>.

Out of all the concert reviews I read, this one seemed the most professional. The writing was eloquent, descriptive, and informative. The writer injected his personal opinion (as one should in a review), but was completely unbiased. I liked that instead of just listing the songs they played, he wrote out a synopsis of the entire concert and included the songs in it. I also liked that he described the crowd's reaction to the concert.

3. Schwenke, Matt. "A dressed down affair." <u>Concert Livewire</u>. 22 Oct. 2007. <u>Google</u>. 27 Nov. 2007 <http://www.concertlivewire.com/brighteyes1.htm>.

This review seemed to be centered mostly around pictures. The review itself was only three paragraphs long, but there were seven pictures to go along with it. I liked the abundance of photos because they made the review more interesting, but it seemed like the photos were the first priority for the writer, and the review was an afterthought. The review was written in third person point of view, so it was more informative than opinionated. I would've liked for the writer to say what he thought about the show, instead of just saying what happened.

4. Blagg, Christopher. "Fall Out Boy feeds shrieking fans 'Sugar'." <u>The Concert Goer</u>. 19 Mar. 2006. <u>Google</u>. 27 Nov. 2007 <http://www.theconcertgoer.com/fall-out-boy-tcgreview 169.html>.

   This was a pretty basic review. The synopsis was brief, and it had all the basic elements of a concert review, but it didn't really elaborate on anything. Good reviews can give you the sense of actually being at the concert, but this one didn't at all. While I was reading it, I felt like the writer could have written so much more. I did like that he compared Fall Out Boy to the boy bands of the 80's and 90's; it's a fair comparison that people who don't pay much attention to music nowadays could relate to.

5. Olsen, Eric. "Concert Review: Modest Mouse At Burton Cummings Theatre, Winnipeg, MB, Nov. 7, 2007." <u>Blog Critics Magazine</u>. 11 Nov. 2007. <u>Google</u>. 27 Nov. 2007 <http://blogcritics.org/archives/2007/11/11/210002.php>.

   This review was particularly extensive. It was one of the longer reviews that I read, and also one of the best. The writer spent a lot of time talking about his personal experiences before and during the concert, regarding the crowd, security, etc. He didn't say much about the opening acts, though. On the flipside, he said a lot about Modest Mouse—what they played, how they played, how they interacted with the crowd, who was in the band, etc. I liked that he evenly split his coverage of the headlining band and the actual concert experience.

6. French, James. "Concert Review—Ben Harper and the Innocent Criminals." <u>Tokyo Weekender</u>. 3 Feb. 1998. <u>Google</u>. 27 Nov. 2007 <http://www.weekender.co.jp/vault/ben harper/ben.html>.

   The first thing that struck me while reading this review was how the writer seemed to neglect using proper grammar and punctuation. Other than that, it was a good review. He included a very comprehensive play-by-play of the concert, giving an extensive report about every detail of the show. He also said what he thought of the performance, which is definitely a necessary element to include in a review, as I have learned.

7. Rake, Jamie L. "Mute Math/Eisley." <u>The Phantom Tollbooth</u>. Oct. 2007. <u>Google</u>. 27 Nov. 2007 <http://www.tollbooth.org/2007/creviews/mme.html>.

   I didn't care much for this review. The writing was incredibly pretentious, so much so that it was to the point where it was hard to understand what the writer was saying, because they used so many long and difficult words. It seemed very calculated—more focus was put on sounding important than giving the reader a clear understanding of how the concert was. This made me realize that concert reviews should be fun to read, in the same way that concerts are fun to attend.

8. Baldman, Anthony. "Ani DiFranco." Folk and Acoustic Concert Reviews. 28 Mar. 2001. Wildplum. Google. 27 Nov. 2007 <http://www.wildplum.org/reviews/>.

Based on the layout of review's website, it appeared that the writer of this review was not a professional concert reviewer. However, upon reading the actual review, I found the opposite may very well be true. The writing was informative and educated, and he even analyzed the political messages behind some of the songs played. This showed me that although the review should be fun, it should also explore the deeper meaning behind the songs.

9. Samudrala, Ram. "Hell Freezes Over Concert Review." Music Ram-blings. 13 Sep. 1994. Google. 27 Nov. 2007 <http://www.ram.org/music/reviews/hell_freezes_over .html>.

This was another review that I didn't enjoy reading. The writer used too much slang, which made him sound uneducated and unprofessional. He also had problems with grammar and punctuation, and used a lot of run-on sentences. It was very irritating to read. He did not seem to write about anything integral to the actual concert, rather, he focused on unimportant details that didn't add anything to his review.

10. Lamb, Bill. "James Blunt, a Fearless Performer." About.com: Top 40/Pop. 21 Oct. 2006. About.com. Google. 27 Nov. 2007 <http://top40.about.com/od/concert1/fr/ jamesbluntconc.htm>.

This review focused a lot on the emotion of the performance, which is something most other reviews I read didn't do. It helped to imagine what the concert was like, and almost put me in the reviewer's shoes. A minor negative detail about this review is that the writer didn't say much about which songs were performed; he only listed about four songs. This helped me because it showed that there has to be a balance between the emotional and informative aspects of the review for the reader to truly appreciate it.

How-to Book

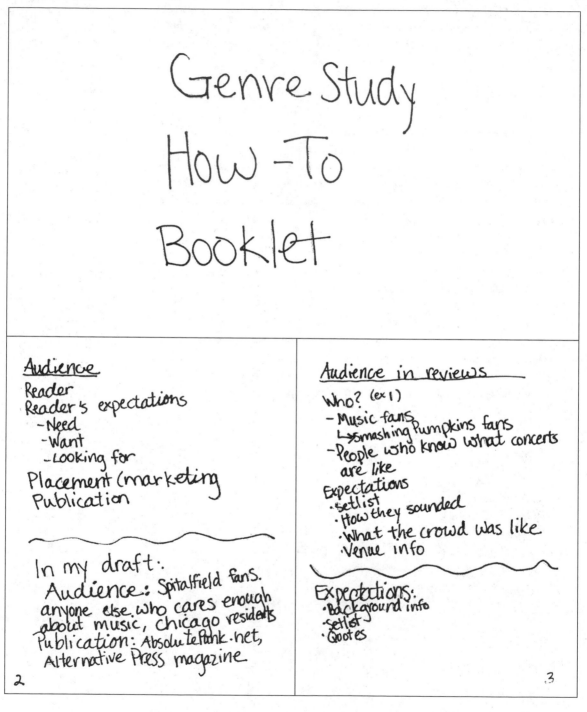

Genre Study
How-To
Booklet

Audience
Reader
Reader's expectations
 - Need
 - Want
 - Looking for
Placement (marketing
Publication

In my draft:
 Audience: Spitalfield fans.
anyone else who cares enough
about music, chicago residents
Publication: AbsolutePunk.net,
Alternative Press magazine

2

Audience in reviews

Who? (ex 1)
 - Music fans
   ↳ Smashing Pumpkins fans
 - People who know what concerts
   are like
Expectations
 · Setlist
 · How they sounded
 · What the crowd was like
 · Venue info

Expectations:
 · Background info
 · Setlist
 · Quotes

3

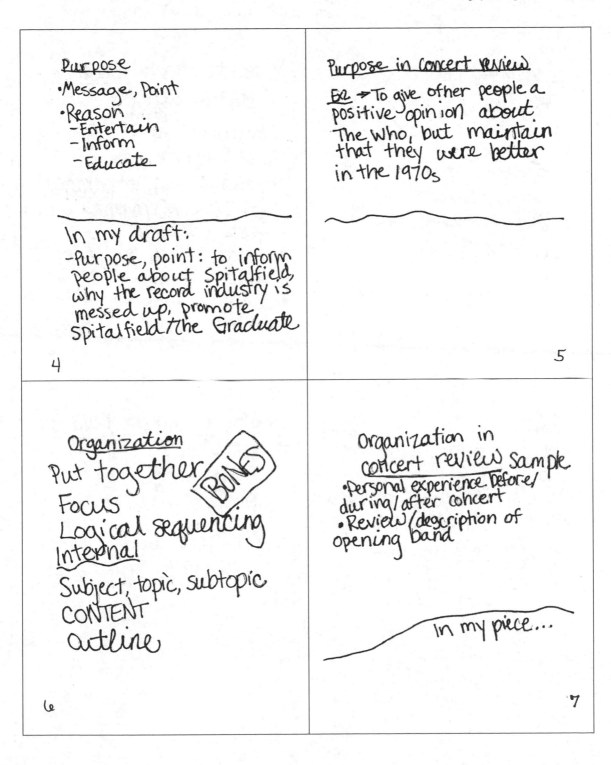

Purpose
- Message, Point
- Reason
  - Entertain
  - Inform
  - Educate

In my draft:
- Purpose, point: to inform people about Spitalfield, why the record industry is messed up, promote Spitalfield / the Graduate

4

Purpose in concert review

Ex → To give other people a positive opinion about The Who, but maintain that they were better in the 1970s

5

Organization
Put together / BONES
Focus
Logical sequencing
Internal
Subject, topic, subtopic
CONTENT
outline

6

Organization in concert review sample
- Personal experience before/during/after concert
- Review/description of opening band

In my piece...

7

Presentation

Shows
Looks like
Columns
Font
Spacing
Headline
Pictures

SKIN

8

Presentation in concert
review sample
online
• Regular font
• Ads along side
• Pictures next to paragraph
• Date of show / name
  — Date published
• Link to more pictures/
  videos at end
• Calendar links to more
  reviews

9

Voice

* Style
* Sounds
* How they express themselves
* Subject matter (content)
* Do you know the writer
  without a byline

10

Voice in concert review
• Laid back
• Fun, free yet
  professional

• Mature but
  relaxed

11

Word Choice

* Words they choose to put together
* Vocabulary
  accessible, simple, high-brow

I don't care whether you can name the problem so long as you can fix it; but I do care if you are completely checked out, or frustrated, or giving up on proofreading.

12

WC in concert review

* Simple, easy to understand
* Some slang

13

Sentence Fluency

* Flow (not choppy)
* Sounding "put together"
* Structure of the
  simple sentences (noun)
  Subjection + action (verb)
* Adds personality/voice
* compound— 1 + 1 + __
* complex
* Combining sentence types

14

Sentences in concert review

In my piece:

15

Proof-reading + Style
· Run-on / comma splice

Because it is so Icy outside,
school officials in Ypsilanti
and Milan declared a snow
day, but Ann Arbor didn't,
We're still in session.

16

Style Issues in Concert
Review

In my piece:

17

Leads 1st or 1st and 2nd ¶
· Beginning
· HOOK → Draws reader
                   in
· Attention grabber

Ex: * quote - really controversial
    * Story-telling
         ↳ Jump into a scene
    * 5 Ws and H
    * Play on words

18

Leads in Concert Review
Sample
   Background details
        (boring)

In my draft:
· Quote announcing
   breakup. Gives background
and explains; sets the
tone for rest of article

19

Letter from an Interested Adult

Dear Julia—

Well, of course I enjoyed your piece on Spitalfield's "Curtain Call" tour. Your words brought back plenty of bittersweet memories for me. You truly captured what it felt like for a fan to see one of her very favorite bands for the last time.

I agreed with your assessments of the various bands' performances, and it helped that you were comparing two shows on the same tour. I was also surprised by how much better Attention was on the second show—boring at their first show, and much more engaging later on. It was a good example of how people can improve with a little experience—and that makes a good metaphor for writing as well. Keep it up, and your skills improve, and it's easier to engage your audience.

Your up-close perspective on the bands was especially instructive. And, of course, reading a bit about Dan's exploits was fun—describing fans' reactions (the girl who was texting during one band's set, and that fight that suddenly broke out at the end of Spitalfield's final performance) adds some perspective to your piece.

Keep up the writing, and let's go see more bands!

Love,

Mom

Evaluation Letter

Julia,

I thoroughly enjoyed reading your music review. I don't even know this band, and I found myself feeling disappointed in their breaking up. One thing your review wasn't completely clear about: What does Spitalfield sound like? I feel like I know more about the other bands' sounds than your feature. That is the only question I had in my head as I read. Throughout, I was pleasantly surprised by your integration of your own concert-going experience with your analysis of the music and performances—it absolutely kept me interested in this quite long article to the very end.

I'm most impressed with your exploration of voice throughout the project. I was surprised to read in your research journal that before our class lesson you "hadn't given much thought to [it] . . . so it was definitely an eye-opener," because your how-to book has notes, but no "application to your own writing" section. You obviously didn't let it go, though, because it is one of your central concerns in your annotated bibliography and the concluding paragraph of your final reflection. Furthermore, the article truly is a nice blend of personal and professional.

Bravo!

Ms. Andrew

P.S. I love that your mom goes to concerts with you!

Rubric

Julia Rosenzweig

NAME *Music Review*

JOURNALISM GENRE RESEARCH PROJECT RUBRIC

Author's Checklist		A 9-10 points	B 8 points	C 7 points	D 6 points	E 0-5 points
	Research journal is thorough (Write an entry each time you work on the project)	12 or more	9-11 entries	6-8 entries	3-5 entries	0-2 entries
	Research journal explains your research process, metacognition and feelings	Insightful	Perceptive	Process addressed	Somewhat addressed	None
	Final piece looks and reads like stated genre	Excellent	Good Job	Average	Little effort	Doesn't look or read like genre
	Final piece is readable, interesting, engaging and enjoyable	Excellent	Good Job	Average	Little effort	Poorly written
	Reflection on final piece (yourself as a reader, writer and researcher)	Insightful	Perceptive	Observant	Somewhat reflective	None
	Conference notes (from parents, peers and teacher, each on own draft)	Plenty	Ample	Sufficient	Few	None
	All drafts and experiments	Plenty	Ample	Sufficient	Few	None
	Collection of (5-10) published samples	Good choices	Representative	Adequate	Poor choices	None
	Annotated Bibliography of model samples (in collection)	Insightful	Perceptive	Observant	Somewhat reflective	None
	Proofreading (final piece and all reflections)	Very few errors	Some errors	Same errors throughout	Many errors	Excessive errors

VERY!

I especially like your discussion of voice.

not labeled, but the notes are good.

Stick with partner

A

chapter

6

Variations on the UGP

ONE THING WE KNOW for sure about teaching: if you want any idea you read about to work in your own classroom, you have to adapt it to fit the context and circumstances that are part of your own reality. And the best ideas we've "stolen" from others have worked well because they are full enough and flexible enough for us to adapt. Orthodoxy, as Nancie Atwell (1998) tells us, is the enemy of good teaching; thoughtful, meaningful, continual adaptation is the only way for new teaching ideas to find true meaning and form in a classroom.

The best compliment any teacher could give our work would be to adapt these ideas about genre study and the Unfamiliar Genre Project for other purposes, in other settings, and in ways we haven't even imagined yet. As we've presented workshops on this project over the past few years, we've always closed with some time for teachers to think about how the UGP might work in their own classrooms, prompting them to consider the circumstances in which they teach, the philosophies they hold about language and language learning, and the curriculum for which they're responsible. We've been amazed and delighted at how many really intriguing ideas have come up, even with just ten minutes of thought and discussion.

In this chapter, we want to share a few adaptations and variations of the project that we have put into practice. While each of them remains true to the essence of the UGP, we believe the variations are great examples of what can be done with this concept of helping students enter new genres—for whatever reasons. We start with Sarah's explanation of how she has adapted the UGP for use in her journalism class and how what she renamed the Journalism Genre Project for that context immersed students in the multiple and varied genres in that field. Next, Sarah writes about another adaptation she has put into practice: her rendition of the UGP as a whole-class study of memoir within a literature course. And we close with what was actually not a variation, but the original conception of the project: Cathy's version of the UGP for preservice teachers.

As you read these renditions, we encourage you to ask that all-powerful teacher question: How would this look in my class? Explore, experiment, and make it your own.

Sarah's Journalism Genre Project: A Journey Through the Genres of Journalism

After our venture into the genre studies described in Chapter 3, I was asked to teach journalism, a class I had not taught in six years. A bit apprehensive at the thought of designing an updated journalism course (so much to teach and never enough time to cover everything), I realized that the way I had taught the composition course—starting with a series of genre studies and building to the Unfamiliar Genre Project—might adapt well to journalism. I could base the initial whole-class studies on different types of journalistic writing, leading up to a slightly revised version of the UGP, which would allow students to explore one of the many other genres of journalism. And for all the reasons that this approach worked in my composition class, it turned out to be a great way to teach journalism.

Teaching journalism classes in the past had shown me that too many students think journalism is going to be fun, right up until the moment they are actually confronted with the reality of journalistic writing. Traditional journalism courses that begin with the inverted pyramid and the various rules of newswriting tend to feel limiting to many students and turn off a number of them before they ever get a chance to see how exciting journalistic writing can actually be. Keeping this in mind, I decided to change things up a bit and begin with something that would be interesting and maybe a little different: a genre study of the editorial cartoon. I prepared for this first genre study over the summer, gathering editorial cartoons from newspapers and magazines, and then spent the first few days of the semester simply immersing the kids in these drawings. As we laughed our way through that immersion and the questions that accompanied our study, the kids soon identified the elements that matter in a political cartoon (many of which apply to journalistic writing as a whole): it should be current, humorous, newsworthy, fact based, with a political edge or point of view. And starting with the cartoons worked out just right: the students learned how to inquire into a genre even as they learned some of the basics of journalism. Best of all, we'd established community—this was going to be fun, creative, and intellectual. They were hooked on the class.

As this two-week foray into editorial cartoons continued, I introduced many of the same minilessons I had used in the comic book genre study: drawing lessons in perspective and facial expressions, literary lessons in archetypes and symbols, and craft lessons in exploding the moment (see Chapter 3). The genre study culminated with students drawing and writing their own political cartoons, some based on school issues, some reaching out to state and national political concerns.

We moved next into our second short genre study, sports writing, timed because Homecoming was fast approaching, and that meant there would be a number of home games that my students could attend (from men's tennis, soccer, football, and water polo to women's field hockey, golf, and volleyball to coed cross-country and crew). I enlisted the athletic director to provide press passes to these budding journalists and prepared even the not-so-sports-minded students for the genre. We brainstormed the vocabulary associated with each sport and the rules for each game, relying on those students who were experts in particular sports. Once prepared, we dove into reading a number of sports articles by some of the best student, local, and national writers, looking for the elements and qualities that make sports reporting its own genre. As the students got more familiar with the genre, I then introduced the notion of interviewing: the reasons journalists rely on interviews, ways to conduct interviews, and strategies to incorporate interviews into the actual writing. We practiced interviewing in class to prepare students for the three interviews required for this project. And despite their initial fears, students approached players, fans, even cheerleaders and then integrated the material into their own sports story in their chosen sport.

Three more genres followed, all with a similar approach to immersion, inquiry, instruction, and integration: reviews, news and features (which we looked at together in order for students to see the similarities and differences between the two), and columns (which turned out to be the students' very favorite).

These five genre studies served as prelude to the Unfamiliar Genre Project, which I renamed the Journalism Genre Project for this class. Set up very similarly to the standard UGP, the Journalism Genre Project began with our looking at a list I provided of all the journalism genres I could think of with the caveat that students had to pick a genre or subgenre they hadn't already tried.

Students then followed the process Cathy and I had devised for the UGP in general: they selected a genre; immersed themselves in it by reading lots of examples; wrote a proposal about their genre; began the process of writing, receiving feedback, and revising; created a how-to book; wrote an annotated bibliography; kept a reflective journal; solicited a letter from an interested adult; and wrote their final draft and reflection.

For the most part, the project proceeded very similarly to other UGPs I have worked on with other students in other classes. (See Figures 6.1 and 6.2 for

JOURNALISM GENRE PROJECT

Picking a Journalism Genre

We'll begin this project with honest soul-searching as you pick a genre that challenges you and expands your knowledge of journalism. I want you to pick a genre that is both interesting and genuinely challenging. This is a research project as well as a writing project. Therefore, the quality of the final piece will account for only a small part of your grade on the project; engaging in the research process and the reflective journal will constitute most of your grade. A proposal in which you identify your journalistic genre along with an explanation of why you chose it and what you'd like to learn is due at the end of class on _____.

Here are some genres you might consider exploring. Don't limit yourself to these!

Consider Your Medium

Internet

newspaper

- *The Emery* (the high school newspaper)
- *The Ann Arbor News*
- *The Observer* (local alternative newspaper)
- *New York Times*
- *USA Today*
- *The Onion*
- other

magazine

- *Time*
- *Newsweek*

- *Sports Illustrated*
- *Teen Vogue*
- *Maxim*
- *Wizard*
- *Rolling Stone*
- other

radio

- National Public Radio
- WJLB
- WJR
- 105.9 KISS FM
  - Tom Joyner in the Morning

television

- morning news
- evening news
- late-night news
- Nick news
- PBS
  - Ken Burns–style documentary
- newsmagazine
  - *Dateline*
  - *Entertainment Tonight*
- talk show
  - *Oprah*
  - *Real Sports with Bryant Gumbel*

FIGURE 6.1. *Journalism Genre Project*

Consider Your Genre

commercial or advertisement	opinion column	review
documentary	personality profile	• book
editorial	political/editorial cartoon	• CD
feature article	science report	• concert
in-depth report	sports	• movie
interview	• article	• play
investigative reporting	• column	public service announcement
literary nonfiction ·	• season wrap-up	photo-essay (with captions)
news article	• interview	
obituary		

Consider Your Audience

teens	video gamers	general public
thirty-somethings	musicians	elderly
parents	children	doctors (trade publications)

Consider Your Purpose

inform (news)	entertain	opinion
educate (consider the *why*)	feedback	

Research Binder

The final project will take the form of a research binder. It should be typed, organized, and easy to navigate. Your binder should include the following (make one tab for each category):

- centerpiece and final reflection (discuss your reading, writing, research process, and metacognition)
- research (metacognition) journal (with dated entries)
- experimental writing, all drafts, and all conference notes
- copies (with reading notes) of the best five to ten samples of published work in your chosen genre, explained in an annotated bibliography

(continues)

FIGURE 6.1. *(Continued)*

JOURNALISM GENRE PROJECT *(Continued)*

- letter from an important adult
- how-to book, constructed in class

The Research Journal

Although research includes many steps, the order of these steps may vary, like in writing. You may want to jump right into a draft. You may prefer to begin by reading (and collecting) samples of your genre. Perhaps you will begin by journaling: you might first deal with your fears toward this unfamiliar genre by putting them to paper. To some extent, this project is intended to allow you to discover your own research process, which you'll write about in your final reflection. Whatever your process, metacognition (thinking about your thinking) is an important part of this research project. Throughout this study, keep a journal (handwritten or typed—your preference) of your experiences. *Use this journal to keep track of your daily activities as well as your feelings about each stage of the work.* You'll write about your metacognition in a section of your final reflection. Write in this journal each time you work on the project.

Reading in Your Genre

One part of your research in this genre study is to simply read within the genre. You must collect the best five to ten samples of published work in your chosen genre that you can find. (This means that you will be reading more than five to ten samples!) Once you've chosen your models, carefully reread them as you think about (and take notes on) the writer's craft, structure, and unique strategies in each piece. You'll create a bibliography listing each of these models along with an annotation for each. Finally, consider what the collection as a whole teaches you about the genre: What are its characteristics? Where are its boundaries? In what ways does this genre borrow from other genres? In what ways do other genres borrow from this? You'll synthesize these big-picture observations in the reading portion of your final reflection.

Annotated Bibliography

An annotated bibliography is a formatted list of your five to ten model samples (bibliography) with a paragraph of thoughtful observations about the way each model sample was written or crafted (annotation). You will write an annotation for each of the model samples you collected for your genre. Notice in the rubric for this project

FIGURE 6.1. *(Continued)*

that your annotated bibliography is worth 20 percent of the project grade. It is important that you pay as much attention to writing your annotated bibliography as to writing your centerpiece (also worth 20 percent of the project grade).

Writing in Your Genre

The centerpiece of this project, of course, will be a finished piece in your chosen (challenging) genre. You must take this piece through several drafts including parent, peer, and teacher conferences (required). Before you actually get to your final piece, it's likely that you'll experiment with the genre—you may have several starts before you write the piece you will finish for your final project. *Keep all of the writing (drafts, false starts, conference notes) you accumulate throughout this project.* As you are writing, be aware of what you are doing: How did you write in this genre? What were your influences? What writer's tools did you use? You'll synthesize these observations in the writing portion of your final reflection.

How-to Book

In class, we'll analyze some aspects of writing: audience, purpose, content, organization, presentation, voice, word choice, sentence fluency, proofreading, and other writing minilessons. We'll keep our notes from this analysis in a how-to book that we'll discuss together, but you will individually track your chosen genre. This how-to book, which will count toward your homework grade during the unit, will serve as a planning tool for writing in your genre and a resource as you write your annotated bibliography.

Reflective Letter

The last piece you'll write for this project is your reflective letter. Consider your experience over the weeks of this project. Reread your journals. Reread your drafts and experimental writing. Reread your notes on your reading. With all this in mind, think about what you've learned about reading in this project. What have you learned about writing? What have you learned about studying genres and researching in general? In your letter, discuss your reading, writing, research process, and metacognition. The purpose of this letter is to make big-picture conclusions from your experience.

Letter from an Important Adult

As you know, I think it's really important to share your hard work with your parents and guardians (or another important adult). When you are completely finished with your Journalism Genre Project, share it with a parent, guardian, or another interested adult and *ask him or her to write a letter to you* after reading your project.

FIGURE 6.1. *(Continued)*

JOURNALISM GENRE PROJECT SCHEDULE

November

Monday	Tuesday	Wednesday	Thursday	Friday
12 Introduction Week **Introduction to JGP:** Highlighter activity **Minilesson 1:** Metacognition and your research journal **Minilesson 2:** Set up research binder, tabs	13 Introduction Week **Idea Workshop** *Proposal DUE* at the end of the period. **To Do Today:** ● Search for, print, and read samples. ● Finish writing proposal.	14 Introduction Week **Minilesson 1:** Identifying *model* samples **Minilesson 2:** Mini genre study: MLA bibliography entries **DUE** by end of the period: one model sample bibliography entry in MLA style.	15 Introduction Week (Substitute today: Ms. Andrew at NCTE) **On Computers:** Continue search online for articles in your genre **To Do Today:** ● Find samples online. ● Print copies. ● Read (immerse yourself). ● Inquire into how each piece was written. ● Add each to MLA bibliography.	16 Introduction Week (Substitute today: Ms. Andrew at NCTE) **To Do Today:** ● Research strategy scavenger hunt **DUE** at the end of the period!
19 Workshop 1 (Substitute today: Ms. Andrew at ALAN) **To Do:** Work on JGP. **My Workshop Plan (computers available):**	20 Workshop 2 (Substitute today: Ms. Andrew at ALAN) **To Do:** Work on JGP. **My Workshop Plan (computers available):**	21 **No school.**	22 **No school.**	23 **No school.**
26 Analyzing Craft Day 1 **Lesson:** News article inquiry (game)	27 Analyzing Craft Day 2 **Checkpoint:** *Bibliography of ten model samples* DUE. **Lesson:** Make booklets, how-to booklet: content v. craft (pp. 1–4)	28 Analyzing Craft Day 3 **Lesson:** How-to booklet: audience and purpose (pp. 5–8) **To Do Today:**	29 Workshop 3 **Minilesson:** What is experimental writing? **My Workshop Plan (computers available):**	30 Journalism law and ethics: *Tinker v. Des Moines*

May be copied for classroom use. © 2009 by Cathy Fleischer and Sarah Andrew-Vaughan from Writing Outside Your Comfort Zone (Heinemann: Portsmouth, NH).

FIGURE 6.2. *Journalism Genre Project Schedule*

December

Monday	Tuesday	Wednesday	Thursday	Friday
3 Analyzing Craft Day 4 **Lesson:** How-to booklet: organization and presentation (pp. 9–12) **To Do Today:**	4 Analyzing Craft Day 5 **Lesson:** How-to booklet: voice and word choice (pp. 13–16) **To Do Today:**	5 Analyzing Craft Day 6 **Lesson:** How-to booklet: sentence fluency, proofreading, and leads (pp. 17–22) **To Do Today:**	6 Workshop 4 **Checkpoint:** Experimental draft **DUE.** **Minilesson:** Confering **My Workshop Plan (computers available):** Conference!	7 Journalism law and ethics: *Bethel v. Fraser*
10 Annotated Bibliography Day 1 **Lesson:** Mini genre study: immersion and inquiry into annotations	11 Annotated Bibliography Day 2 **Minilesson:** Writing annotations **To Do Today:** ● Write your annotations.	12 Review Sample Projects 1 **Lesson:** Analyze strengths and weaknesses of sample projects	13 Review Sample Projects 2 **Checkpoint:** Annotated bibliography **DUE.** **Minilesson and To Do:** Analyze strengths and weaknesses of your (and classmates') projects	14 Journalism law and ethics: *Hazelwood v. Kuhlmeier*
17 **Project** Workshop 3 **Minilesson:** Organize your binder, tabs **My Workshop Plan (computers available):**	18 Workshop 4 **Minilesson:** Writing your final reflection **My Workshop Plan (computers available):**	19 Workshop 5 **Minilesson:** Proofread your project! **My Workshop Plan (computers available):**	20 Workshop 6 **Minilesson:** Asking an important adult for a reflective letter **My Workshop Plan (computers available):**	21 **Journalism Genre DUE** Read and write a reflective letter to *three* classmates. IF YOU ARE ABSENT, YOU MUST TURN THE PROJECT IN EARLY (BEFORE BREAK)!

FIGURE 6.2. *(Continued)*

the introductory handout, including the list of genres, and the unit calendar. The rubric remains similar to the general one described in Chapter 4.) However, one difference in student learning that really jumped out at me was how students truly came to understand the immediacy of purpose, audience, and medium for journalistic writing. Of course, they had heard the lesson before (from me and a host of other teachers): "All writing is connected to audience, purpose, situation, medium." But perhaps because most of their writing is school writing, in which these considerations are pretty set in stone, it can be hard to convince students of the truth of this message. Once they were truly immersed in their journalistic genre of choice, however, almost every student noted that it was impossible to write in that genre without considering the context. A feature article for a teen magazine, they found, has some similarity to but is clearly not the same as a feature article for the *New York Times Magazine*. The tone changes, the diction changes, the syntax changes, even the paragraph structure and content change. Because journalistic writing is so integrally tied to audience and publication, students were suddenly taking note of the variations within a genre in new ways. They were amazed by the differences they noted, and I was amazed at their increased understanding of the underlying complexities in the concept of genre.

My first foray into transferring the UGP almost wholesale to another content area convinced me of what Cathy and I imagined as we were devising the UGP: the transfer to other subjects and disciplines is not only possible but holds great potential for all kinds of teaching and learning. I can imagine reading and writing across the curriculum in which teachers and students explore the genres inherent in their subjects. As I envision teaching courses in creative writing or speech, for example, I see how this approach might enhance my work. And in Michigan, where all English classes are required to demonstrate an integration of writing, reading, listening, speaking, and viewing, I can think of no better way of integrating English language arts curriculum than through the Unfamiliar Genre Project!

Sarah's Whole-Class UGP: Looking at Memoir

Another adaptation I made to the UGP emerged from a course my school names Short Readings (which for some students is code for "I've never liked an English class and I probably won't like this one either"). Teaching this yearlong course for the first time, I spent the entire first semester trying to help students feel good about being in an English class—or at least better than they had before––by encouraging them to believe in themselves as readers and writers, by inviting them to experience what real readers and writers do, and by offering them great choice in their reading and writing. In short, I instituted an almost total reading-writing workshop in which we had reading days, writing days, daily minilessons, and lots of feedback through peer and teacher conferences. And the students responded very positively. While they needed a lot of support throughout the semester, they reported that they were reading much more than they ever had before and were starting to feel confident in themselves as writers.

As second semester approached, I struggled with what to do to further push my students' growth. Would it be possible, I wondered, to try the Unfamiliar Genre Project with these students who had been so turned off by traditional English classes? Would the momentum of the first semester be lost? Would they be able to handle the independent nature and the rigor of this project?

Buoyed by the success of the UGP in some other class settings, I decided to give it a try, realizing that I would have to make some adaptations to really have it work. The variation I ultimately came up with was a whole-class UGP—a project in which we would together select a genre and adapt the UGP process to that whole-group focus. This, I thought, would be a middle ground: introducing the students to the kind of independent research that is the hallmark of the UGP with additional support along the way.

We began the process of selecting a whole-class genre with a lot of talk. I explained that we'd just spent a whole semester in which they got to do a lot of individual work in what might be called familiar genres, they'd had the opportunity to choose the genres that felt comfortable to them and then select the topics they wanted to write about. But now we would all study a genre together, I told them, one that may be less comfortable for them as individual writers but one that they would choose as a class. I then offered them a choice of three genres: poetry, memoir, and short story (genres I knew would allow me easy access to a lot of material and that I thought would be of interest to the class). After some wonderful classroom battles, the students opted for memoir, although some of the advocates for poetry were disappointed in this choice. Drawing on that moment, I promised them I would include some poetry in the unit, thinking immediately of some poems that read as memoirs. This spur-of-the-moment promise actually led to one of the key learning moments of the unit: Could poetry be memoir? Do some poems fit under that umbrella? How are the lines drawn in various genres? Memoir, it turned out, was a perfect choice for what became a complicated and important discussion about the nature of genre, especially in terms of those pieces that sit on the edges of mainstream definitions.

We began, as we do all UGP units, with immersion and inquiry into the genre, reading together a host of selections from various memoirs I love, including, as promised, some poetry that reads like memoir: Patricia Smith's "Building Nicole's Mama," Theodore Roethke's "My Papa's Waltz," Ann Bradstreet's "An Author to Her Book," Langston Hughes' "Cross," Sylvia Plath's "Daddy," and Paul Lawrence Dunbar's "Incident." We even explored whether songs could be memoirs as I played a song written and recorded by my stepfather; students were then quick to bring in their favorites. Together we read short selections from books like *I Know Why the Caged Bird Sings*, by Maya Angelou; *Me Talk Pretty One Day*, by David Sedaris; *The Woman Warrior*, by Maxine Hong Kingston; *Night*, by Elie Wiesel; *All Over but the Shoutin'*, by Rick Bragg; and *Bird by Bird* by Anne Lamont (some of which are called memoir and some of which are called autobiography), as well as small excerpts from the slave narratives *Narrative of the Life of Frederick Douglass*, by Frederick Douglass, and *Incidents in the Life of a Slave Girl*, by Harriet Jacobs. We complicated our discussion with bits from semiautobiographical works such as *The Bell Jar*, by Sylvia Plath, and Robert M. Pirsig's *Zen and the Art of Motorcycle Maintenance*.

I told them the story of my search to find a copy of *The Woman Warrior*, years after I had read it in college, becoming baffled when I couldn't find it in the fiction section of the bookstore. Eventually, I learned it was classified under autobiography, and I was shocked. That book, written so movingly with all the narrative techniques I associated with fiction, was actually memoir? And this, of course, led us down a path of discussion: How is memoir like and unlike fiction? What are the differences between these two genres? At this point, I drew upon the fine line we were discovering, by introducing the idea of fiction that reads like memoir, inserting excerpts from texts such as *The House on Mango Street*, by Sandra Cisneros, and *The Things They Carried*, by Tim O'Brien, that furthered our discussions of the differences and similarities among fiction, poetry, lyrics, autobiography, and memoir as we worked hard to characterize which was which, increasingly understanding that the lines demarcating this genre are pretty shaky.

All this wonderful (and, to be frank, pretty unexpected) discussion led us down another, slightly different yet fascinating avenue as we thought about James Frey's "memoir," *A Million Little Pieces* (2003). How should we characterize this piece that was marketed as memoir but turned out to be at least partly fictional? I brought in newspaper articles and a video of Oprah Winfrey on *The Larry King Show* and students were thrust into the controversy about what is essentially a literary discussion: What is it that makes something one genre rather than another? This perfect moment of integration across genres occurred: What is this genre all about and where are the lines drawn? What characteristics of fiction should transfer to memoir and what shouldn't? What is a genre, anyway?

As we had a lot of in-class discussion of memoirs we read together, I asked students to select at least one memoir to read individually, giving them one class period a week to read. In preparation for this, I went to the school librarian and asked for every memoir she had; I brought the books in on a big cart and gave kids time to browse and then choose. Some kids still chose from their home library, and many relied on recommendations from friends. Wonderfully, some books started making the rounds, being passed from student to student. Some popular that semester were *The Freedom Writers' Diary*, by Erin Gruwell and the Freedom Writers, *Bad Boy*, by Walter Dean Myers, *Black, White, and Jewish: Self Autobiography of a Shifting Self*, by Rebecca Walker, and *Boy*, a memoir by the much-beloved children's author Roald Dahl. (See Figure 6.3 for a complete list of books students read that semester.) What resulted from this individual reading is what you might expect and what I hoped would happen. It was impossible to keep our class discussion of genre separate from the outside reading these teens were doing, and, in fact, they kept bringing to our class discussions their insights from their individual books: Did the books demonstrate the characteristics we were coming up with for memoir? Were there differences? How did individual authors use craft to bring the reader into their life story? Were there techniques that the students might want to try out in their own writing?

While we were doing all this reading, students began writing their own memoir, based on some incident in their own life, following pretty much the pattern of the Unfamiliar Genre Project. (See Figure 6.4 for a partial schedule of the project.) We had read a lot of samples together, pulling them apart as we identified the characteristics, and students wrote annotated bibliography entries on these group readings as well as their individual books. As a whole group, we also put together the how-to book, focusing on the characteristics of memoir and illustrating it with observations from their individual reading. The rest of the project proceeded individually: students kept a reflective journal about their reading and writing; they composed their own memoir; they conferred with parents, peers, and me; and they wrote a final reflection.

The final pieces demonstrated unbelievable growth for so many of the students; their writing came alive, and they took great pride in their work. Happily, the class ended with a mutual warmth toward English, reading, and writing, and each other; I feel strongly that the Memoir Genre Project was instrumental in this achievement.

MEMOIRS AND AUTOBIOGRAPHIES
STUDENTS READ INDEPENDENTLY

(collected from student reading records, March–May 2007)

Black, White, and Jewish: Autobiography of a Shifting Self, by Rebecca Walker

Boy: Tales of Childhood, by Roald Dahl

The Abracadabra Kid: A Writer's Life, by Sid Fleischman

I Know Why the Caged Bird Sings, by Maya Angelou

The Million Dollar Mermaid, by Esther Williams

Candy Girl: A Year in the Life of an Unlikely Stripper, by Diablo Cody

Nothing: Something to Believe In, by Nica Lalli

Lunar Park, by Bret Easton Ellis

A Child Called It: One Child's Courage to Survive, by Dave Pelzer

The Lost Boy: A Foster Child's Search for the Love of a Family, by Dave Pelzer

All Over but the Shoutin', by Rick Bragg

Bad Boy: A Memoir, by Walter Dean Myers

Blowing My Cover: My Life as a CIA Spy, by Lindsay Moran

When I Was Puerto Rican, by Esmeralda Santiago

Every Second Counts, by Lance Armstrong with Sally Jenkins

Son of a Grifter: The Twisted Tale of Sante and Kenny Kimes, the Most Notorious Con Artists in America, a Memoir by the Other Son, by Kent Walker with Mark Schone

Yes I Can: The Sammy Davis Jr. Story, by Sammy Davis and Jane and Burt Boyar

Tony Hawk: Professional Skateboarder, by Tony Hawk with Sean Mortimer

On Writing: A Memoir of the Craft, by Stephen King

The Autobiography of Malcolm X, as told to Alex Haley

The Freedom Writers Diary: How a Teacher and 150 Teens Used Writing to Change Themselves and the World Around Them, by the Freedom Writers and Erin Gruwell

Wasted: A Memoir of Anorexia and Bulimia, by Marya Hornbacher

Between a Rock and a Hard Place, by Aron Ralston

Black Bird: A Childhood Lost and Found, by Jennifer Lauck

Falling Hard: A Rookie's First Year in Boxing, by Chris Jones

FIGURE 6.3. *Memoirs and Autobiographies Students Read Independently*

No Name in the Street, by James Baldwin

White Is a State of Mind: A Memoir, by Melba Pattillo Beals

Running with Scissors: A Memoir, by Augusten Burroughs

Me Talk Pretty One Day, by David Sedaris

Dress Your Family in Corduroy and Denim, by David Sedaris

Naked, by David Sedaris

Angela's Ashes, by Frank McCourt

'Tis, by Frank McCourt

Teacher Man, by Frank McCourt

Zlata's Diary: A Child's Life in Wartime Sarajevo, by Zlata Filipovic

Finding Fish, by Antwone Q. Fisher and Mim E. Rivas

Ultra Marathon Man, by Dean Karnates

Invincible: My Journey from Fan to NFL Team Captain, by Vince Papale and Chad
    Millman

October Sky: A Memoir, by Homer Hickman

Dispatches from the Edge: A Memoir of War, Disasters, and Survival,
    by Anderson Cooper

Naked in Baghdad, by Anne Garrels

African Nights, by Kuki Gallmann

My Life, by Bill Clinton

The Only Girl in the Car, by Kathie Dobie

Michelle Kwan: Heart of a Champion—an Autobiography, by Michelle Kwan and
    Laura M. James

90 Minutes in Heaven: An Inspiring Story of Life Beyond Death, by Don Piper with
    Cecil Murphey

Gemini: An Extended Autobiographical Statement, by Nikki Giovanni

Ophelia Speaks: Adolescent Girls Write About Their Search for Self, edited by
    Sara Shandler

High Tide in Tucson, by Barbara Kingsolver

I Feel Good: A Memoir of a Life of Soul, by James Brown and Marc Eliot

*Giant Steps: The Remarkable Story of the Goliath Expedition from Punta Arenas to
    Russia*, by Karl Bushby

Dreams from My Father: A Story of Race and Inheritance, by Barack Obama

FIGURE 6.3. *(Continued)*

MEMOIR GENRE PROJECT SCHEDULE
(AFTER STUDYING MEMOIRS AS A WHOLE CLASS)

April

Monday	Tuesday	Wednesday	Thursday	Friday
23 **At the Library** • Introduction to memoir study (read the overview). • Find a memoir. • Set fourth quarter goals.	24 **Lesson:** MLA works cited and annotation of excerpt from *I Know Why the Caged Bird Sings* **Class Work:** Reading as MLA entry	25 **Reading Workshop:** Timed reading **Lesson:** Can lyrics be memoir? Kevin's song. **Calendar:** Make a plan for this unit.	26 **Reading Workshop:** 30 minutes **"No ideas but in things":** Adding concrete objects to writing	27 **Reading Workshop** Calculate reading grade (×3).

May

Monday	Tuesday	Wednesday	Thursday	Friday
30 **Reading Workshop:** Timed reading **Lesson:** from *Me Talk Pretty One Day*	1 2nd hour: Junior class meeting **Lesson:** Snapshots **Workshop To Do:**	2 **Lesson:** Thought shots **Writers' Group:** Bring a draft of your memoir. (CHECKPOINT!)	3 JUNIORS: Pen Pal letter DUE. (Introduce yourself; you're starting the exchange. Include copies of all your memoir assignments.) **Lesson:** Dialogue **Workshop To Do:**	4 **Reading Workshop** Calculate reading grade (×6).
7 **Reading Workshop:** Timed reading **Lesson:** from *Bird by Bird*	8 **How-to Book:** What is said (content) v. how it is said (craft) **Workshop To Do:**	9 **How-to Book:** Content, organization, and presentation **Writers' Group:** Bring a draft of your memoir. (CHECKPOINT!)	10 JUNIORS: Pen pal letter DUE. **How-to Book:** Voice, word choice, and sentence structure. **Workshop To Do:**	11 **Reading Workshop** Calculate reading grade (×9).

FIGURE 6.4. *Memoir Genre Project Schedule*

Monday	Tuesday	Wednesday	Thursday	Friday
14 **Reading Workshop:** Timed reading **Lesson:** MLA entries and annotations revisited	15 **Lesson:** Check your draft against your how-to book **Workshop To Do:**	16 **Lesson:** Sensory details **Writers' Group:** Bring a draft of your memoir. (CHECKPOINT)	17 JUNIORS: Pen pal letter DUE. **Lesson:** Final reflection **Workshop To Do:** **POETRY SLAM TONIGHT**	18 **Reading Workshop** Calculate reading grade (×12).
21 **Memoir Project DUE for Seniors**	22 **Lesson:** Can film be memoir?	23 **Lesson:** Can film be memoir? (continued)	24 JUNIORS: Pen pal letter DUE. **Lesson:** Presentation **Workshop To Do:**	25 **Reading Workshop** Calculate reading grade (×15).

May be copied for classroom use. © 2009 by Cathy Fleischer and Sarah Andrew-Vaughan from Writing Outside Your Comfort Zone (Heinemann: Portsmouth, NH).

FIGURE 6.4. (Continued)

155

Cathy's Original Unfamiliar Genre Project: How Do We Teach Empathy?

> This genre was truly challenging for me and I can understand now how difficult it would be for my students to write in a genre they are unfamiliar with. I think when teaching any unit in writing the most important aspect to emphasize is practice makes perfect. Kids will not produce a perfect piece of writing on their first try, especially if they are writing a type of literature that they either do not like or do not know. Encouraging students, much like you encouraged us in class, that the most important part of writing is at least attempting it was very helpful.

Amy wrote these words just after completing her first attempt at an ode, a genre she recognized as a big challenge to her. And for me, these words were a perfect reflection of what I hoped my students, preservice English teachers, would start to understand about the UGP.

How did Amy (and a host of others—five years' worth of students now) get to that point? Here's how it starts in my class:

"OK, let's get going," I call over the beginning-of-the-class conversation in my Writing for Writing Teachers course. "Today we're going to start on the project you've been hearing about all semester: the Unfamiliar Genre Project. For this project I'm going to ask you to trust me and to do something that I know is really hard: choose to write in a genre that you don't feel so good about. Maybe you've heard about the genre before but don't know much about it. Maybe it's a genre that you've tried before but the result wasn't so great. Maybe it's a genre that you're actually really excited to try but just haven't had the opportunity to before."

I pause for a breath and look around at the faces of the twenty-four pre-student teachers staring back at me, most of them showing the signs of apprehension I've come to recognize as a normal part of the journey I'm about to ask them to undertake. These students, soon to be English teachers, consider themselves to be writers and, from what I've learned in years past, are successful in part because they stick to the path of writing that good English majors have followed for years: they know how to summarize, analyze, and cite in order to write excellent literary analyses; some of them have even ventured into poetry and creative writing; a few have some journalistic background and are skilled in feature and newswriting. I know they're asking themselves a good question: Why should they take the leap out of their safety zone into writing something that makes them uncomfortable?

I continue on. "Let's think for a minute about the students you'll soon be teaching. How many of them do you think love English the way you do? How many of them think of themselves as writers? How do you think they'll feel when you ask them to write something that is so easy for you now but may be unfamiliar or uncomfortable for them?" They look interested as I pause again. "OK, that's the main motivation behind this project: I want you to experience what it feels like to be a student who is asked to write something that is difficult. I want you to think about what you'll do to learn a new genre, what strategies help you, where the process slows down and even shuts down, how you dig yourself out of the holes." I can see in their eyes the question that's lurking there for these students accustomed to getting As and Bs in their English classes. "And here's where you really have to trust me," I add. "I really do want you to pick a genre that's hard for you, not to fake it and pick one that you are already good at but that you pretend is hard in order to get a better grade." A few hesitant laughs and furtive looks at each other. "But no one was planning to do that, right?"

I continue, "I really do mean this and to prove it to you, let me tell you about the grading of these projects. I actually don't care what the final genre reads like. I don't care if it is pretty bad. What I care about, and what I'll grade you on, is the attempt at understanding a new genre, your improvement over various drafts, and—most of all—your reflection on the process."

Again, we pause. "Let's take five minutes and jot down some ideas about what genre you might want to write in and why. Then we'll share."

And so we begin this process that has truly revolutionized my teaching of this course. (See Figure 6.5 for the student handout I distribute.) The class, a required course for anyone receiving a secondary teaching certification in English at my university, introduces students to the teaching of writing through a double-pronged approach: as students are immersed in their own writing projects, they also learn about research-based best practices for teaching writing; it's a delicate balancing act for those of us who teach it as we continually nudge the students toward being very self-conscious about their own writing experiences in hopes of their connecting those experiences to the various teaching strategies they're learning about. They get used to us saying, after we try out a certain approach or strategy to help them in their own writing, "OK, now take off your student hat and put on your teacher one. How could you adapt what we've just done for a classroom of fifteen year olds?" Students are introduced to a genre-based approach to teaching writing, for example, as they compose a literacy memoir that recounts some particular experiences in writing; as they work on that writing, we focus on both the concept of genre study and particular ways of teaching revision. As they work on their own memoir, they try to put into practice some of those strategies for revision, pausing along the way to consider how those work for them as writers. At the same time, we talk about how they might use these strategies in their own teaching.

UNFAMILIAR GENRE PROJECT FOR PRESERVICE TEACHERS

Writing in Your Unfamiliar Genre

The goal here is to choose a genre that is challenging to you—either because you've tried writing in it before and had difficulty or because you've never had the opportunity to write in that genre. Coming to understand the genre a little more, then, is one of your goals. In order to complete this part of the assignment, you should begin by writing a proposal to me that identifies the genre, your reasons for writing in that genre, and what you hope to learn by pursuing that genre. You will then write several drafts, get feedback from your peers and me, and write a final version.

Investigating Your Unfamiliar Genre

In order to feel more comfortable in the genre, you'll need to learn something about it. You should pursue your learning in that genre in two ways: (1) collect some examples of the genre that you really like (at least four to six samples) and (2) try to find at least one teaching article (from a journal or a book) that talks about writing in that genre—either an article that specifically talks about how to teach students to write in that genre or one that talks about how to go about writing in that genre. (This step is designed to have you begin to create the kind of genre file that Atwell talks about in her book.) Immersing yourself in the genre by reading examples—by trying to read as a writer—will help you when you begin writing. For much of the next few weeks, your major reading assignment will be to read in that genre.

Remember as you do your reading that no genre is pure. In this project you are not trying to reach a cookie-cutter definition of your genre; rather, you should look for all the complications of style, form, language, and so on that surround

May be copied for classroom use. © 2009 by Cathy Fleischer and Sarah Andrew-Vaughan from Writing Outside Your Comfort Zone *(Heinemann: Portsmouth, NH).*

FIGURE 6.5. *Unfamiliar Genre Project for Preservice Teachers*

your genre. Genres are complex entities, and raising questions about the genre is an integral part of this assignment.

Reflecting upon Your Unfamiliar Genre and Your Research Process

The reflection consists of three parts: a *journal* you keep as you immerse yourself in the genre, a *how-to book* in which you demonstrate to others what you've learned about the genre, and the final *reflection* you will write based on the journal.

- *Journal:* Think of the journal as an informal place to keep track of what you are learning about the genre and your progress in your writing. You should write in it every time you spend some time on this project. Entries can summarize what you're learning from your reading, have prewriting moments, reflect your feelings about the writing, begin to summarize the key points you've discovered about your genre, include responses to your peers' critiques, and so forth.
- *How-to Book:* The how-to book is designed to be shared with your peers: a short book that will help other prospective teachers understand more about the genre. It should explain the genre (e.g., What would someone need to know in order to really understand this genre? Is there variation within the genre?), list the defining characteristics of the genre, and provide references for samples of the genre (i.e., you don't need to include the actual samples here, but you should have a short bibliography and/or links that others can use to find samples). This will be posted on the CoLEARN site.

(continues)

FIGURE 6.5. *(Continued)*

UNFAMILIAR GENRE PROJECT FOR PRESERVICE TEACHERS
(Continued)

- *Final Reflection:* In order to write this reflection, you should ask yourself questions like these: What about writing in the genre was challenging? What was easy? What helped push me through? What have I learned about the genre (from my writing experience and from my immersion in the genre)? What have I learned about teaching writing in that genre? This final reflection should be three to four pages.

Teacher's File

The final draft that is handed in to me should be in the form of a *teacher's file* and should include the following:

- four to six samples of the genre
- your teaching article
- a copy of your how-to book
- your actual writing, including all drafts and the final piece
- a three- to four-page final reflection

Remember, your grade for this project will be based on the whole teacher's file—not only on the piece of writing!

May be copied for classroom use. © 2009 by Cathy Fleischer and Sarah Andrew-Vaughan from Writing Outside Your Comfort Zone (Heinemann: Portsmouth, NH).

FIGURE 6.5. *(Continued)*

The Unfamiliar Genre Project fits perfectly into this way of thinking about writing and writing pedagogy for many reasons. First and foremost, it helps the college students experience themselves what it means to write something that is outside their comfort zone. Let's face it: the group of students who choose to major in English and become English teachers is pretty self-selecting. Not many of them get to this 400-level course without feeling fairly comfortable with themselves as writers. It's easy for these students to forget (if they ever actually experienced) what it feels like to be scared to write or to have that panicky moment when they have no idea what to do when a teacher assigns some kind of writing that seems just impossible. Just experiencing that moment has been eye-opening for my students. They realize, first of all, how complicated it is to write something that isn't already a part of their repertoire. They try to write a sonnet and get so focused on the rhyme scheme that they find themselves losing meaning. Or they attempt a news story and find they're not able to express themselves as they're used to because of the condensed nature of the undertaking. Or they choose a genre, like picture book, that seems simple enough on the surface but becomes increasingly complex the more they study it: who the audience is (The kids or the parents? What age child?); what the purpose is (To entertain? To put forth a moral? To educate?); what all the subgenres are (poetry, nonfiction, fiction, etc.).

Students reach different levels of discomfort and even frustration during the process, and so I ask all of them to keep reflecting on what they're going through as they immerse themselves in the genre and eventually write their own version of it: What are the stopping points? How do they work their way through the dilemmas? What happens to their writing as a result of the frustration? And even as they wear their student hat, I ask them to constantly put on their teacher hat, to consider what this kind of frustration might be like for their future students.

This act of struggling through a genre leads my students to increasingly appreciate what it must be like to be a student writer who has never been all that successful at writing. When my students struggle through this one piece, they have a lifetime of success and confidence to draw upon—as well as a battery of strategies that have helped them in the past, strategies they can usually transfer from a beloved genre to this new one. Even with that confidence, though, they often produce a piece that doesn't meet their standards. They soon come to realize that if the genre is hard to figure out, the writing that results is often not so good. And this is what leads to their second big aha moment, this one about the students they will someday teach: perhaps as their future high school students are introduced to new genres, their actual writing may not be so great at first. Once that realization takes hold, my preservice teachers are much more understanding toward the writing of high school students, recognizing in the high school student papers they review the same kinds of struggles they have just faced.

I can't overstate what a big deal this is for my students and for me. Year after year I struggle with the way too many of my novice teachers react to the examples of high school students' writing I share with them in hopes of preparing them for the reality of assessing and commenting on writing, especially the writing of struggling students. Over and over, many view this writing from a deficit model, talking about everything these students don't know and how unprepared they are. Far too many of my students seem to be able to focus only on the "mistakes." Once I ask these college students to attempt to write in a genre that is uncomfortable for them and they find themselves in the position of struggling to produce something they can be proud of, they begin to realize how complicated it is to write well when you are unfamiliar or uncomfortable in a genre. They realize that their own writing in this case is not particularly strong and that it is peppered with "mistakes." They worry about sharing it with others, concerned that their peers will see it as horrible; they forget about all kinds of commonplaces in terms of punctuation, spelling, and formatting as they focus so hard on getting the genre right; they sometimes just give up and either abandon the project or do the minimum to get it done. In short, they learn a lot about teaching, a lot about why students might respond to writing assignments in certain ways, and a lot about the nature of error in writing.

Equally important, they learn some good specific pedagogical lessons: about creating a supportive atmosphere where students can ask questions, about having some flexibility to abandon a project if it truly isn't going well, about introducing certain constructs in writing a few at a time, about how teachers can help writers be successful.

Another value of this project has been the opportunity it offers preservice teachers to expand their repertoire of genres. As we've stressed throughout this book, no writer can be familiar with all the genres that are out there. And no teacher can be expert in all genres. For many of us this presents a challenge, especially when we use a writing workshop approach and students compose in genres that just aren't in our experience. How do we help the student who is writing a microfiction if we've never attempted that genre? How can the advice we give be worthwhile if we've never struggled through that genre's goal of telling a story, making that story emblematic, and keeping words to a minimum? Even though we can't know all the nuances of every genre, some familiarity on our part can really help students. When we know, for example, some of the characteristics of one-act plays, we can help a student think through how to try on that genre. When we understand the complexity of haiku, we can help a student do more with it than just count syllables and try to find words that fit.

This project offers novice teachers a chance to gain some expertise in multiple genres in two ways. The first, of course, arises from their deep immersion in the genre they choose. By the time they finish with this assignment, they have read deeply in the genre, thoughtfully struggled with the differences and similarities they've noticed in the examples they've gathered, developed a list of characteristics of the genre (with appropriate qualifications about the genre), thought about ways to introduce students to it, written their own example of it, and reflected on the process of that writing. By the end of the process, they know quite a bit. However, they also gain at least some expertise by sharing their learning with others in the class. The culmination of this project is a teaching file that includes their attempt at the genre, a written statement about the genre describing its qualities and characteristics as well as variations within the genre, a collection of interesting samples of the genre, and a reflection on the project as a whole. More recently, I've stolen and adapted the idea of the how-to book; my students now create a booklet (of any design: I've had students who wrote brochures, pop-up books, as well as more traditional how-to books) that explains to others how to approach this genre, a booklet I hope my students will share with their students someday. Each of my students then posts this teaching file online for the others in the class. I encourage them to read and download one another's files in order to create their own collection, so that when they begin in their own classroom, they will have excellent materials for themselves and for their own students. In a typical semester my students have access to twenty to twenty-five files, usually representing at least fifteen different genres: a great collection with which to begin their teaching lives.

The way we achieve all this is not so different from what Sarah does with her high school students, adapted for a college class that meets only once or twice a week (depending on the semester) and that can focus on this project for only three to four weeks. My students choose a genre of interest, immerse themselves in that genre, write a proposal for how they'll proceed, keep a reflective journal about their journey, and write their own rendition of the genre. In class we engage in minilessons about various aspects of genre study, both procedural and craft based, and students have time to confer with each other and me on their writing. Additionally, because I am able to work so closely with Sarah, my students have the benefit of seeing how the UGP looks in a high school class as I share many of the lessons Sarah uses and examples of the finished projects. Some semesters my students even exchange UGP drafts with their high school pen pals in Sarah's class, giving and receiving response and encouragement.

Recently a former student stopped by my office to report on his just-completed student teaching experience. As we talked about the highs and lows of his semester, he excitedly told me about the way he used the UGP in his own classroom. "It was different," he explained, "but it really worked for the middle schoolers I was teaching." He joined the ranks of a host of new teachers who report to me that they're trying the UGP out in their own classrooms: adapting it for their students, their context, their needs. Beginning with their own experiences in our methods classes, these apprentice teachers are learning a new way to teach English—and we couldn't be happier.

Bibliography

Andrew-Vaughan, Sarah, and Cathy Fleischer. 2006. "Research Writing: The Unfamiliar Genre Project." *English Journal* 95 (March): 36–42.

Atwell, Nancie. 1998. *In the Middle.* 2nd ed. Portsmouth, NH: Heinemann.

Bakhtin, Mikhail. 1986. "The Problem of Speech Genres." In *Speech Genres and Other Late Essays,* translated by Vern W. McGee, 60–102. Austin: Univ. of Texas Press.

Bazerman, Charles. 1997. "The Life of Genre, the Life in the Classroom." In *Genre and Writing: Issues, Arguments, Alternatives,* edited by Wendy Bishop and Hans Ostrom, 19–26. Portsmouth, NH Heinemann.

Berthoff, Ann. 1981. "Reclaiming the Imagination." In *The Making of Meaning,* 23–29. Portsmouth, NH: Boynton/Cook.

———. 1987. "The Teacher as Researcher." In *Reclaiming the Classroom: Teacher Research as an Agency for Change,* edited by Dixie Goswami and Peter R. Stillman, 28–38. Portsmouth, NH: Boynton/Cook.

Bloom, Bengamin S., Bertram B. Mesia, and David R. Krathwohl. 1964. *Taxonomy of Educational Objectives.* New York: McKay.

Bomer, Katherine. 2005. *Writing a Life: Teaching Memoir to Sharpen Insight, Shape Meaning—and Triumph over Tests.* Portsmouth, NH: Heinemann.

Bomer, Randy. 2003. Foreword to *Thinking Through Genre: Units of Study in Reading and Writing Workshop, 4–12,* by Heather Lattimer. Portland, ME: Stenhouse.

Freedman, Aviva, and Peter Medway, eds. 1994. *Learning and Teaching Genre.* Portsmouth, NH: Boynton/Cook.

Frey, James. 2003. *A Million Little Pieces.* New York: Doubleday Books.

Gere, Anne, Leila Christenbury, and Kelly Sassi. 2005. *Writing on Demand: Best Practices and Strategies for Success.* Portsmouth, NH: Heinemann.

HAIRSTON, MAXINE. 1982. "The Winds of Change: Thomas Kuhn and the Revolution in the Teaching of Writing." *College Composition and Communication* 33 (February): 76–88.

HERRINGTON, ANNE, AND CHARLES MORAN. 2005. "The Idea of Genre in Theory and Practice: An Overview of the Work in Genre in the Fields of Composition and Rhetoric and New Genre Studies." In *Genre Across the Curriculum,* edited by Anne Herrington and Charles Moran, 1–20. Logan, UT: Utah State Press.

———, EDS. 2005. *Genre Across the Curriculum.* Logan, UT: Utah State Press.

JOHNS, ANN M., ED. 2002. *Genre in the Classroom: Multiple Perspectives.* Mahwah, NJ: Lawrence Erlbaum.

KITZHABER, ALBERT R. 1990. *Rhetoric in American Colleges 1850–1900.* Dallas: Southern Methodist University Press.

LANE, BARRY. 1993. *After the End: Teaching and Learning Creative Revision.* Portsmouth, NH: Heinemann.

LATTIMER, HEATHER. 2003. *Thinking Through Genre: Units of Study in Reading and Writing Workshop, 4–12.* Portland, ME: Stenhouse.

MCCLOUD, SCOTT. 1993. *Understanding Comics: The Invisible Art.* New York: Harper Collins.

MICHIGAN DEPARTMENT OF EDUCATION. 2006. *English Language Arts Grade Level Content Expectations.* michigan.gov/documents/ELAGLCE_140483_7.pdf (accessed March 18, 2008).

MILLER, CAROLYN. 1984. "Genre as Social Action." *Quarterly Journal of Speech* 70: 151–67.

NATIONAL COUNCIL OF TEACHERS OF ENGLISH (NCTE). No date. *Writing Matters: A Collection of Resources and Strategies for Creating a Quality Writing Program to Support Adolescent Literacies.* Urbana, IL: NCTE.

PUTZ, MELINDA. 2006. *A Teacher's Guide to the Multigenre Research Project: Everything You Need to Get Started.* Portsmouth, NH: Heinemann.

ROMANO, TOM. 2000. *Blending Genre, Altering Style: Writing Multigenre Papers.* Portsmouth, NH: Heinemann.

RUSSELL, DAVID R. 1997. "Rethinking Genre in School and Society." *Written Communication* 14 (October): 504–55.

ST. JARRE, KEVIN R. 2008. "Don't Blame the Boys: We're Giving Them Girly Books." *English Journal* 97 (January): 15–16.

SPANDEL, VICKI. 2001. *Creating Writers: Through 6-Trait Writing Assessment and Instruction.* New York: Wesley Longman.

SPIEGELMAN, ART. 1986. *Maus: A Survivor's Tale.* New York: Pantheon Books.

WILSON, MAJA. 2006. *Rethinking Rubrics in Writing Assessment.* Portsmouth, NH: Heinemann.

Also Available

BLENDING GENRE, ALTERING STYLE
Writing Multigenre Papers
Tom Romano

Blending Genre, Altering Style is the first book on the practicalities of multigenre papers. Tom Romano discusses genres, subgenres, writing strategies, and stylistic maneuvers that students can use in multigenre papers.

Romano works with classic genres such as poetry, fiction, and dialogue. He also shows how students can create genres out of indelible moments, crucial processes, and important matters inspired by the subjects of their papers.

Suffused with Romano's trademark passions for teaching and writing and supported with numerous student examples, *Blending Genre, Altering Style* is an invaluable reference for any teacher with a desire to help students write well in any genre—or several of them.

978-0-86709-478-7 / 2000 / 208pp / $22.00

Sample Chapters available online at www.heinemann.com

Heinemann
DEDICATED TO TEACHERS

To place an order, **call 800.225.5800,** or **fax 877.231.6980.**